Harrison Moore

CREDIT REPAIR AND CREDIT SCORE SECRETS

A Complete – 2 in 1 – Guide

Learn how to Restore, Repair and Improve your Credit Report and Protect Yourself from Creditors and Banks using Federal Laws and How To Raise Your Credit Score Quickly and Get Rid of Bad Credit

Table of Contents

Harrison Moore

CREDIT REPAIR

SECRETS

Introduction

Credit repair is a term that is utilized to allude to the procedure/methods taken or applied so as to transform an awful credit report into a decent one. This repair procedure, otherwise called restoration, should be possible by erasing negative/wrong data from one's record and finding a way to change one's costs so as to raise one's score. The demonstration itself is otherwise called fixing one's credit.

The motivation behind restoration is basic - it is done so as to keep and maintain a decent monetary life without awful evaluating and to such an extent that it will be anything but difficult to move toward budgetary foundations for loans such that one will be affirmed. In any case, it doesn't end there.

A second reason for restoration or fixing is to improve one's chances of getting good financing costs on loans with the end goal that it will be simpler to reimburse over the long haul.

In any case, the need to fix or repair one's document and increment the score is additionally ensuing on different components. These incorporate the need to find a new line of work, advancement, or to carry on with a more joyful life. For example, the number of bosses who presently utilize the record as a device for deciding how qualified a new position candidate is continually expanding every day. In a similar vein, a few bosses likewise utilize their representatives' reports as an appraisal instrument when thinking about advancing some staff in an association.

Taking a gander at these reasons, it turns out to be progressively obvious that there's no avoiding fixing/repairing a terrible record so as to endure the day by day battles individuals will undoubtedly involvement in accounts, especially when making long haul arrangements for a home loan or school reserves.

To reestablish an awful report, all you need do is to contract a specialist credit repair organization to do it for you, or basically do-it-without anyone's help. The do-it-without anyone else's help strategy is getting more grasped by individuals, particularly the individuals who have sufficient opportunity to experience all the procedures in question. In any case, this is best finished with the guide of a restoration-kit/manual. Continuously guarantee you get an ongoing duplicate of your 3-in-1 document before you begin fixing.

Chapter One

What Does Credit Repair Mean?

Great inquiry! It's the basic procedure of "fixing" one's credit by utilizing the accessible buyer credit laws to encourage the evacuation of negative things. The law most much of the time utilized (and referred to) is the Fair Credit Reporting Act (typically called the FCRA) and the entirety of the corrections and modifications made to this law throughout the most recent a very long while. (practically restrictive for the CONSUMER... which is a decent thing..:-)

Is credit repair lawful?

Totally. What's more, the law above promises it also. The straightforward truth is that while there are numerous deceitful individuals on BOTH sides of the credit fence (loan specialists, sellers, and repair offices the same), the key option to challenge, contest and REMOVE things from your report is 100% , genuine or more board for sure!

For what reason does the credit fix business have such an awful name?

Reality? Since there is such a lot of cash on ALL sides. What's more, since credit is such a significant product from numerous points of view... that pioneering individuals of various kinds and stripes have searched out to exploit the credit tested. This incorporates savage lenders as well as credit repair "centers" that frequently guarantee to "fix" your credit medium-term, utilizing techniques that are sketchy, best case scenario... out and out illicit at the very least.

Is credit restoration even conceivable?

Indeed, beyond a shadow of a doubt. Truly, I've actually utilized an assortment of basic, extremely direct, and effective credit repair techniques on my own reports on MORE than one event. (also, giving myself "A" credit in under 4 months, when it began as a "D"... or then again even an "F" time and again) The credit laws are set up, in all honesty, to FAVOR you and me, and beyond a shadow of a doubt, presently is the absolute best time to figure out how to fix your credit after all other options have been exhausted!

Can I repair my credit myself, or do I need to hire a company to do it for me?

Great question - and you can ABSOLUTELY fix your credit yourself. No company is required, although arguably, those who have more professional experience may, in fact, be able to help you get better results faster SIMPLY because they have already learned the landscape. (not much different than a plumber can fix your pipes faster than you may!)

What is the Credit Repair Organizations Act?

Are you considering enlisting a credit repair facility yet only somewhat reluctant about your privileges, your cash and

Whatchance that anything they can accomplish for you all things considered?

Think about what! You are not the only one. Credit repair is a huge business. What's more, there are numerous trustworthy, dedicated assistance experts who fastidiously and determinedly will work to assist you with expelling negative things from your credit record. Obviously, in the notorious yin and yang that our radiant free undertaking economy brings to the table, there are additionally PLENTY of fleeting, corrupt, ill-equipped, and out and out obscure administrators with a bad reputation that will take your cash and not do a thing for you.

Hence, congress enacted the Credit Repair Organizations Act to guarantee there was an unmistakable, reasonable, and handily intervened set of rules that illuminate, in genuinely explicit detail, what a credit repair organization can, and can't do to get your business. It additionally explains how they may charge you (no longer forthright), what sort of terms they can stipulate, and how and when you may demand a discount on the occasion, you would prefer not to seek after the procedure after welcoming them on.

While many credit repair firms have endeavored to go around a portion of the numerous arrangements in the law, and the understandings set out by the Federal Trade Commission on its application, the bottom line is you are MUCH.

More secure today than you were 10 or 12 years back on the off chance that you need your FICO to score kneaded to improve things. Most firms won't chance a protest and strive to guarantee they are giving you the administration and stipends the law orders. It is additionally imperative to recollect that credit repair is splendidly lawful. By excellence of there existing a law that polices the business, you ought to likewise comprehend that by definition, that should crush those naysayer's including some credit department writing) that will propose that reestablishing your credit by employing an expert firm is disagreeable, or far more detestable - ILLEGAL! It most unquestionably isn't don't as well, stress - countless individuals like you and I have profited incomprehensibly from holding their administrations. A couple of rotten ones can ruin the bundle - however, do your due perseverance, comprehend your privileges, and the vast majority of all - get that credit score fixed and do it soon! Life is unreasonably short for awful credit. Stop! They are LYING their backside's off about YOUR credit score!

What is the Importance of the Credit Repair Organizations Act?

Anyone who is looking for the administrations of a credit repair organization is qualified for some fundamental rights. Regardless, the administrators of these administrations ought not to request any installments until and except if the administrations guaranteed have been rendered. The Credit Repair Organization Act (CROA) is sure about what comprises assistance most definitely. The Act likewise plainly expresses the segments of a legitimately restricting contract.

If the conditions set on the contracts are not regarded, at that point, no installments ought to be made. Clients can cancel the contract singularly with no punishment being forced on them. This is the most impressive arrangement of the Credit Repair Organization Act, undoubtedly. He should, in this manner, utilize it each time the contract gives off an impression of being a formula for a super million trick.

The Act stipulates that it is your entitlement to be given the fundamental reports that are going to upgrade your comprehension of the law. The contract should be carefully recorded as a hard copy with the goal that it is acceptable in an official courtroom should you have any lawful concerns later on.

The Act additionally depicts in incredible detail what your privileges and commitments are as a customer of credit revamping administrations. For the shopper to be ensured by the Act, he needs to focus on each statement in the Act. This may here, and there be incomprehensible, attributable to the fact that not all individuals who counsel credit modifying organizations are specialists. Right now, Act gives a decent establishment to you to counsel the administrations of legal counselors at whatever point this is important.

The CROA likewise denies organizations from intentionally giving data that is misdirecting, off base, or bogus. This empowers customers to get equity when they are cheated into marking an outrageous contract. As indicated by the Act, each organization must give all the fundamental contact data in the contract. This data ought to be right. A nitty gritty depiction of the considerable number of administrations that the customer needs to be rendered and the period inside which this will be accomplished ought to likewise be remembered for the contract.

Last Tip: The initial step to get your credit report fixed and your scoring improved is getting a credit report from a standout amongst other Credit Reporting Services in the market. For the most part, since it'll show your credit scores and credit repair organizations request it on all occasions, exploit the free preliminary offers and less expensive costs offered, this permits you to check it more than once every year your rating and credit documents. When you get your credit report, take as much time as necessary to locate a respectable credit repair organization.

What Is FICO Score and Why Does It Matter?

FICO is actually the name of a firm (it's an abbreviation; the firm was formerly called the Fair, Isaac Company, started by a designer, Bill Fair and also a math wizard, Earl Isaac. FICO is a company which concentrates on credit history and other analytics for monetary solutions suppliers. Consequently, consumer credit ratings are typically referred to as FICO scores, also when ratings are actually supplied to customers or potential lenders by an additional entity.

FICO has its own proprietary formula for computing credit scores, although it is recognized that payment past history, length of credit past history as well as credit application are all elements which go into calculating this rating. Also reduced of a score as well as you may find it all yet impossible to acquire a car loan of any type of kind; or at the very least, any kind of financing you'll be supplied will certainly be on remarkably unfavorable terms, specifically in regards to passion rates.

When making a decision whether or not you're a appropriate risk, prospective lenders look at your rating. A greater score implies that lending institutions will certainly view you as extra most likely to repay loans promptly as well as in full; simply puts, they'll assess you as a lesser risk.

Your FICO score is expressed as a 3 figure number which may vary anywhere from 500 to 850. A breakdown of these number ranges as well as what they mean follows:

720-850: This is the highest feasible FICO score array; if your credit score falls under this wide range, you'll normally have a simple time receiving a home loan or various other car loans and also will get one of the most beneficial rates of interest as well as other terms and conditions.

700-719: Dropping simply below the 720-850 wide range will certainly still allow you to obtain financing effortlessly and also you'll additionally have the ability to get beneficial terms and conditions on mortgage as well as other kinds of customer funding.

675-699: This is what is typically related to as suitable credit. You'll likely have the ability to get a loan, although you will not obtain terms and conditions which are as favorable as those you would certainly obtain if your credit score was in the 700-719 or 720-850 varieties.

620-674: If your FICO score is in the 620-674 wide range, you'll probably have difficulty getting excellent terms on a loan; and some lenders could determine that you're as well much of a credit risk to extend funding to in any way.

560-619: Customers with credit ratings between 500 as well as 619 will usually have problem acquiring credit as well as will normally pay substantially higher interest prices than will certainly folks with higher FICO scores.

500-559: If your credit score is in the 500-559 wide range, it's not likely that you'll be able to obtain any type of kind of funding; rather, your priority must be to repair your credit score to make sure that you can certify for a home loan or various other funding in the future.

If you're seeking to improve or maintain your FICO score, it is essential to recognize more about just how your score is determined. The following 5 categories are known to be component of the formula used for computing credit ratings, detailed in order of relevance:

- Payment Past history - 35 %.
- Quantity of Financial obligation - 30 %.
- Length of Credit report - 15 %.
- New Credit - 10 %. Types of Credit - 10 %.
-

FIX CREDIT EXPRESS is certified and bonded credit consultants to resolve financial challenges that hinder your credit goals. Credit profile improvements are essential efforts to enable you to have better choices in life. Our credit education services remove negative items off credit reports, while providing free credit education with membership to empower your leverage.

We raise credit scores by working legally and ethically with you, your financial institutions and the credit bureaus to eliminate unfavorable things and errors from your credit report and include positives.

Our advanced software program system allows us to successfully manage your account while utilizing our expertise to establish an action strategy for your time constraints as well as goal.

How to Fix Your Credit Yourself

You can pay a credit repair company to repair your credit, but if you're willing to take a position some time rather than your cash, then you'll roll in the hay yourself without having to pay knowledgeable. The sole questions you would like to understand before you start are what proportion some time is worth to you, and the way comfortable you're with initiating and managing multiple credit profile related contacts via phone and email. You'll also get to be satisfied with reading and writing quasi-legal documents. You'll find example correspondence online, which may assist you with this.

Step 1: Obtain Your Credit Reports

Your credit score is predicated on a mixture of things and knowledge which is reported about you by 3rd parties to the three major credit reporting agencies. The leading agencies we are concerned with are Experian, Equifax, and TransUnion. These three companies are those who are liable for publishing information about you onto your credit report. However, they're not those responsible for generating knowledge. A creditor, a set agency, or another company (known as data furnishers) will tell Experian, Equifax, and TransUnion what to publish about you, and then the credit bureaus will publish it. They are doing not perform a radical investigation into the legitimacy of the knowledge once they initially report it. Only it's discovered and disputed by you'll it's investigated, at which point it's going to are damaging your credit for months or years. It's also quite common for information to vary on each of your three credit reports, which is like playing Russian roulette whenever your credit pulled if you do not fix all three at an equivalent time. The rationale is because you never know which report your potential landlord, employer, or loan provider goes to tug. Let me offer you an example:

You have never checked your credit reports or felt the necessity to try to do so, however, two years ago, a MasterCard account was fraudulently opened in your name, maxed out, and never paid on. You've got never heard anything about it. The MasterCard company, which defrauded, only reports payment information to Equifax and TransUnion, to not Experian. You've got previously approved for an automobile loan from your bank about nine months ago, so you assume your score is sweet. However, you're turned down within the final stages of your employment application and receive a form within the mail stating that a consumer report utilized in the adverse determination of your employment application. Meaning that albeit your bank pulled your Experian information to verify your creditworthiness for your automobile loan, your potential employer used Equifax or Transunion and assumed the fraudulent negative MasterCard entry was valid.

Situations almost like the above are quite every day, and whether you're turned down for a loan, a MasterCard application, employment, or an apartment, it's an enormous disruption to your plans and maybe a stress-inducing severe event. Go and check your credit reports immediately, then once a month from here on call to nip this potential problem within the bud.

The first step to require is to quickly obtain a credit report from each of the agencies above. Legally you're allowed to try to do this for free of charge once per annum, and also whenever you're denied credit or suffer another adverse qualifying event supported the results of a consumer report. To urge your free reports, attend annualcreditreport.com, and follow the instructions to get your report. This is often the official government website for obtaining your free credit reports, and it doesn't require a MasterCard or any quite subscription or trial. Some people aren't ready to receive their reports from annualcreditreport.com, thanks to problems verifying their identity or other reasons. If you're unable to get your reports from annualcreditreport.com, you'll either search online for credit report providers; otherwise, you can contact the credit bureaus directly yourself. Typically you'll find providers online, which can charge you $1 for your first month of access to your credit reports and a credit monitoring service, with the cost rising to about $30 per month after that. Remember, it's free for you if you'll get your reports from annualcreditreport.com, so that is undoubtedly your first choice. If you cannot get them there, try a paid provider or contact the bureaus directly either online or by mail and persuade them to supply you with a replica of your report. I always send mail certified, signature required, with a tracking number - and that I highly advise you are doing an equivalent. Keeping an in-depth record of all of your communications with each entity you'll be contacting is of the utmost importance to your success. The dates of your mailings and of the correspondence you receive as a result are significant. Below are the online addresses for the credit bureaus - search their site or search online for instructions for requesting access to your credit report if you're unable to try to do so through annualcreditreport.com.

So, just to be clear:

annualcreditreport.com - official site for obtaining your credit reports - go here first

Experian.com - Equifax.com - TransUnion.com; contact directly if needed

OK, I've received my credit reports within the mail, or I've accessed them online - now what?

Step 2: Reviewing Your Credit Reports for Accuracy

Once you receive your reports, you'll get to review them for accuracy. Check all carefully. There are several sections you'll get to review, and every one contains important information about you, which of them are going to be checked by employers, landlords, utility companies, your telephone provider, and in fact, potential creditors et al. Credit reports from the three agencies each look slightly different, but are generally composed of sections almost like these:

Personal Profile: This section contains your personal information, like your legal name, your current and former addresses, your employment history, and your birth date.

Credit Summary: A snapshot of your credit, including what percentage accounts are opened in your name and their total balance. Reported delinquencies are going to be listed here also.

Public Records: the chances are that you merely likely do not have any public records listed on your report, but they're quite common. Mistakes during this area of your report also are reasonably common and wish to be disputed immediately. This sort of data includes bankruptcy, tax lien, court records, judgments, and support payment.

Credit Inquiries: Any company you've got permitted to review your credit file (called a robust inquiry) are going to be listed here for two years. Quite 3 questions listed during this section can lower your credit score. If you see companies listed during this section that you simply haven't authorized to tug your credit, then they have to be removed. If you check your credit (such as through a paid provider or credit monitoring service like referenced above), your credit score won't be affected. This sort of inquiry understood as a soft inquiry. Typical listings during this section include lenders, and potential or former employers and landlords.

Account History: this is often the precise account information for all accounts opened in your name, which reported to a credit reporting agency. This information is usually positive or negative and collectively has the most critical impact on your credit rating. An outsized amount of inaccurate information often found on some people's credit reports during this section. Positive information reported about you'll remain on your report indefinitely, while contrary information will stay for 7 - 10 years from the date that the account closed, or the time you last made a payment on or acknowledged the alleged debt.

The contact information for all the businesses who are listing information about you'll even be found during this section. These addresses are where you'll be sending your dispute letters if you select to mail them versus filing online (recommended).

The above sections will comprise the bulk of your credit reports. As stated before, undergo them very carefully. Pay special attention to the alleged amounts that you simply owe, the payment dates, and, therefore, the names of the businesses which are reporting the negative information. Note of whether or not it's the first creditor or a debt collector as this may have an impact on the wording of the letters you'll be sending out, an appearance at the account creation dates. In short, undergo and verify that every single data point which is being reported about you thereon credit report is accurate. Make notations of what you think to be incorrect, reconcile this information together with your records, and if it's not precisely the same, then it's going to be being misreported and hurting your credit profile.

Step 3: First Contact

Now that you simply have reviewed your credit reports, the fun part starts. You would like to require all of the knowledge which you would like to be faraway from your report and start writing letters to deal with those issues. You'll put multiple issues on each note. However, I never send quite three points per letter to any agency and that I recommend you do not either. You'll want to send a message to every of the credit bureaus, which details explicitly the explanations the knowledge should be faraway from your report. If it's inaccurate in any way, then legally it must be faraway from your report. Carefully word your dispute letter with diplomatic and professional language, and inform the credit reporting agencies that you simply want them to research the points you raise in your message as you're disputing their accuracy. If you've got evidence supporting your claim, submit a replica together with your dispute letters. The credit agencies want to report correct information, and that they will check out the evidence you send to them. Confirm you are doing not acknowledge that the debt is yours or make any payment offers as this might potentially restart the seven-year clock that the debt is going to reported about you.

After you've got disputed your items, the credit agencies are allowed a minimum of 30 days to reply under the Fair Credit Reporting Act (FCRA). During this point, they're going to contact the info furnisher and plan to verify the accuracy of the debt they're reporting about you. Generally, the info furnisher will simply respond that the info is correct, and zip will change. The agency will send you a letter explaining that they reviewed your claim, and therefore the information was reported to be accurate, and thus they're going to still say it. If you've got submitted proper documentation supporting your position, the agency will review it. However, they'll always side with the info furnisher and refuse to get rid of the wrong items(s) from your report.

If this happens, you will need to contact the original creditors and the collections agencies if they are involved and request validation of the debt they are reporting about you. Typically you will receive some sort of report generated by them, which simply states that they a certain amount of money. This amount will rarely correlate with what you think you owe, or what is being reported onto your credit report. Depending on what type of information you receive from the data furnisher directly, you may be able to simply write a new letter to the credit bureau with copies of the information you received from the data furnisher and an explanation of how the information doesn't correlate with what is being reported on your credit report. They are also required to be able to validate your debt. This is different than verifying it, which is what data furnishers sometimes do. Look up this distinction online and then check to make sure that they have provided the evidence legally required of them to continue reporting information about you.

The parties you will be contacting include:

The three major credit bureaus

Experian

Equifax

TransUnion

The data furnishers

Original creditors

Collection agencies

Attorneys

Others various parties

Dealing with each of these contacts and correctly generating effective correspondence to them, along with corroborating evidence, will be the best and fastest way to fix your credit reports.

Do not enter into any payment negotiations with collections agencies or any other data furnishers without express written statements from them that they will be deleting the "tradeline" once you have fulfilled your payments. This is a very important step when dealing with data furnishers, and forgetting to specify this could cause negative information to stay on your report for much longer in the form of a paid collections account.

Step 4: Raising or Establishing Your Credit Worthiness

If everything looks good on your credit reports and your score still isn't as high as you think it should be, or if you are just new to obtaining credit, there are several things you should be aware of.

Some credit scoring models will give you a lower score for credit card limits or loans, which are under $2,000 - get a limit at least this high if you can.

The average age of all of your combined accounts is important - the older, the better. What this means is that if you have 10 accounts with an average age of 22 years and then you go out and open 4 new accounts to try and raise your score, the average age of your accounts will drop to just under 15 1/2 years old.

This will have a negative effect on your credit score and may offset any benefit of opening 4 new accounts, which will also generate 4 new hard inquiries, which will also have a negative effect. Make sure you absolutely need credit before applying for it.

Having over twenty accounts in good standing can raise your score. However, the average age of your accounts will generally make more of an impact on your score than the total number of your accounts (see above).

If you have bad credit or no credit - try this out: Pull your credit reports and fix everything on them that you can so that your credit history is as favorable as possible. Save up $200 dollars, and then go to your bank or go online and find a company that offers secured loans and credit cards - these are generally easy to be approved for because the credit limit is the same as the amount which you deposit. In this case, you will deposit $200 to obtain a secured loan; then, you will take the $200 from your loan and open a secured credit card. This way, you will gain two new accounts that are reporting your timely payments to the credit bureaus for the price of one. Also, you aren't really out any money because even though you deposited $200 to obtain a secured credit card and loan, you now have $200 worth of credit at your disposal. Make sure you make timely payments on these two accounts, and your score can easily go up 75 points or more in just a few months. If you can manage a $2,000 secured loan, then you will get the benefit of having a loan and a credit card with credit limits of at least $2,000 each, which will both report to the major credit bureaus and can raise your score even more. If you decide to do this, make sure your secured card provider reports to all three major credit bureaus - and try to pay off your credit card in full each month.

On-time payments to your accounts in good standing are the best way to raise your score and keep it there.

If you are offered a lower credit card limit than you want, you can always call the financial provider and request a higher limit. Sometimes all they need is a little additional information to approve you for thousands of dollars more.

The amount of your credit limit which you actually borrow matters; your debt to credit ratio is what credit agencies use to quickly see how much of your available credit you are using each month. This amount can change on a daily basis and has a major effect on your credit score. Keep the total amount of your debt down to about 20% or less of your available credit to look favorable.

Don't max out individual cards; if you have $10,000 of total credit on three cards of $4,000, $5,000, and $1,000 dollars, don't max out any individual card. Keep each of them at 20% or less utilization to save on interest and to keep your cards from being individually over-utilized.

Keep your cashback by paying your cards in full each month. As long as the accounts are active and being used, paying them off each month won't look bad for your score. By not carrying a monthly balance, you will avoid paying interest completely while still receiving cash back for using your cards. In this case, you can actually make money by properly managing your credit cards if you are disciplined.

Paying twice can save you thousands; many loans can be paid off much quicker by simply taking the monthly amount owed, splitting it in two, and paying it off in two separate payments each billing cycle. If you can add just a little extra in each payment, your savings could be significant, and it could speed up the time it takes to pay off your loan by months. Mortgages and car loans are great for this strategy.

Improve Your Credit Regardless!

At one time, many, numerous years prior, you could experience existence secretly your personality, your credit history, your open records, or having individuals keeping an eye on your life.

Not all that today!

Appears just as today, everybody realizes all they have to think about you: your personality, your credit history, your open records, or the individuals making requests about you. This would all be able to be accredited to PCs, the web, and the "advanced world" we live in. What's more, of course.......... Credit Companies!

Did you realize your credit score and obligation picture all assume significant jobs in accomplishing your money related objectives? Your credit score and obligation picture really have an influence in the entirety of the accompanying:

Moneylenders may utilize your credit score for advance choices and terms in advance. The advanced the credit score, the lower the financing cost.

Home loan organizations may utilize your credit score to choose whether or not you can get an advance and the financing costs they set.

Insurance agencies can choose whether or not you get protection and the rates that concern you.

Proprietors may utilize your credit score to decide if they lease to you, the lease they charge, and the security store the request.

Credit card organizations may utilize your credit score to acknowledge or decrease your application and furthermore decide the loan fee.

So you can undoubtedly observe why with a sound score and capable past credit conduct, you will make it more probable for moneylenders to offer you lower financing costs on the things we referenced above and a lot more preferences that favor you. Knowing your score and how it looks at along these lines turns out to be significant!

Much increasingly significant is:

- Knowing the data and steps you need by and by to address your credit report.
- Realizing where to go and what to do to improve your credit score.
- Realizing how to address your credit score in as quick a period conceivable.
- Realizing how to expel negative things from your credit report.
- Realizing how to depend on yourself as opposed to another person to repair your credit score

You might be thinking, "why not employ somebody to repair my credit report?" Or, "why not go straightforwardly to the credit authorities?" Or, "why not simply let time fix my credit report?" Or "exactly what amount of distinction can my credit make?"

Credit Repair Services may sound fascinating, yet in reality, they might be substantially more difficult than they are worth. They may intentionally haul out their administrations to charge you more. Additionally,in light of the structures you should acquire and round out are muddled, you may very well also have done it without anyone's help.

Books to incorporate printed books, digital books, or sound projects; may likewise solid tempting, yet even the best of them expect you to work your own letters and make sense of for yourself how to best question negative things. Likewise, exceptionally confused!

Credit Bureau Instructions may likewise appear to be luring. However, they could be equivalent to "the wolf educating the sheep!" They might be free, yet you get what you pay for! "Purchaser, Beware!"

One of your objectives ought to be to discover and recognize a program that will help you in Repairing You Credit Score!

The chance that you are searching for a total downloaded PC program for credit repair search for one, which tells you the best way to do it without anyone else's help. Simply be certain they offer:

1. Basic, quick, and compelling methods for improving your credit score.

2. Genuine point and snap effortlessness without any letters to compose, no laws to comprehend, without any entanglements at all.

3. Customization of letters, effectively composed particularly for you with answers to credit agencies in a basic productive way.

4. Quick track "strategies" that can really deliver brings about only days.

5. A computerized contest tracker program customized for your necessities.

6. A "self-coordinated" framework that permits you to invest less energy than you would on the off chance that you paid for help or a lawyer.

Projects can be found on our site. To become familiar with credit repair, follow our connection to the area on Legal, and you will be satisfied to gain proficiency with the means important to repair your credit score.

How To Dispute Your Credit Report Errors

Your credit report contains significant data about you. It, for the most part, incorporates facts about your distinguishing proof information, your bill-paying propensities, requests, and open record data.

Credit departments incorporate and offer your credit data to organizations, which use it to assess your credit applications. In this way, it is significant that your credit report contains total and precise data.

Under the Fair Credit Reporting Act, you reserve the options to dispute the culmination and exactness of data in your credit records.

On the off chance that you discover data in your credit record that you accept is incorrect; what you have to do is to finish the uncommon examination demand structure that accompanies your credit report. Adhere to the structure's directions to round out all of the fundamental data.

You may likewise need to append a letter to your finished structure, dated and marked by you, and alongside duplicates of any documentation you have that demonstrates the blunder in your credit report.

The documentation may incorporate duplicates of dropped checks, deals receipts, account proclamations, or past correspondence among you and the creditor in question.

Joining a letter to the examination demand structure is constantly a smart thought on the off chance that you don't believe that the credit agency's examination structure gives you enough space to clarify why you think there is a mistake in your report.

Keep a duplicate of your finished examination demand structure, letter, and reinforcement documentation. They give you the records of what you said and when you said it. Likewise, the date of the letter will tell you when you ought to have heard back from the credit departments.

When you have finished the examination demand structure, mail it, alongside your letter, and duplicates of any documentation. Send it by confirmed mail with a solicitation for an arrival receipt. At the point when you recover the marked receipt, document it with the remainder of your credit record data.

At the point when a credit agency gets a dispute, it must research and record the ebb and flow status of the disputed things inside a "sensible timeframe," - somewhere in the range of 30 and 45 days, except if it accepts the dispute is "unimportant or unessential."

With that, the credit department can't confirm a disputed thing, and it must erase it.

On the off chance that your report contains mistaken data, the credit authority must address it.

In the event that a thing is deficient, the credit department must finish it.

On the off chance that an examination doesn't resolve your dispute, the Fair Credit Reporting Act grants you to record an announcement of up to 100 words to clarify your side of the story.

The credit department must remember this clarification for your credit report each time it sends it out. Credit agency workers frequently are accessible to assist you with the wording of your announcement.

Know, in any case, that when negative data in your report is exact, just the progression of time can guarantee its evacuation.

Credit agencies are allowed by law to report liquidations for a long time and other negative data for a long time.

Likewise, any negative data might be accounted for uncertainly for use in the assessment of your application form:

- $50,000 or more in credit;

- an extra security arrangement with a face measure of $50,000 or more;

- thought for a vocation paying $20,000 or more.

Chapter Two

How Much Do Credit Repair Services Really Cost

In the desperation to repair their credits as soon as possible, often people avail credit repair services from different companies around the world. By this, they get the advantage of saving time and also utilizing the experience of the professionals of the service providing company.

However, availing such services is almost equivalent to outsourcing the tedious task of legal application for removal of inaccurate entries from your credit account and paying them for the same. Thus, these services are kind of expensive compared to the costs incurred if one undertakes all the procedures on his own.

Lexington law is the most famous and trusted credit Repair Company of all time till date. It has all sorts of schemes that let you increase your credit score 50, 100 or 200 points. Moreover, all the proceedings of this company are completely legal. It is operated by a group of attorneys. It also helps you forward applications for reporting dispute in your credit accounts.

The cost of credit repair by through Lexington law varies depending upon the kind of task that they are doing for you. To open an operating relationship with the Lexington law, the initial sign up charges are $99. Besides that, in order to avail very basic services and consultancy, the Lexington law charges you $39 as a monthly fee. So the total amount of money you pay depends upon the amount of time your credit repair takes. The Lexington law has the concept of monthly charges. Thus, there is no additional fee for any number of disputes and there are no other hidden costs.

For availing some of the premium services offered at Lexington law, the charges are obviously different. There are "Concord programs" that promise you improved results and a faster credit repair. It requires an additional $20 per month to avail the "Concord Standard" service. The concord standard program has features like handling various targeted legal and goodwill interventions, catering to escalated information requests, debt validation in accordance to Fair Debt Collection Practices Act etc.

Another program called the "Concord Premium" provides you with a monthly report on your credit score improvement analysis, in addition to the normal and "Concord Standard" services. It also has features like "Reports Watch (TM)" which is a service that alerts you as soon as it detects any changes in your credit account. This facilitates a close watch on your credit score. "Inquiry Assist (TM)" caters to addressing complex enquiries regarding credit repair. This facility is requires an initial registering fee of $99 with monthly charges of $79.

These are the prices of the most renowned companies in the field of credit repair. It is known for its reliability and legality. Paying this amount takes a huge burden off your shoulders, and your credit score future definitely lies in safe hands. You can however also find other much cheaper or more expensive companies in the market and avail there services. But it is always advised to do thorough research in the background of a company before hiring them.

Just the FAQ's on Credit Repair Services

If you have bad credit and are looking for ways to improve it, you probably have a lot of questions about the best way to get the ball rolling. In this article we'll cover the top frequently asked questions about credit repair and professional credit repair services. By the end of the article you'll have more information you can use to begin repairing your credit.

Q: Isn't it true that you can't change what is on your credit report, so credit repair services can't really do you any good?

A: No, that is a myth. The Fair Credit Reporting Act states that you can contact the credit reporting agencies and dispute negative items on your credit reports. Any information that you feel may be incorrect, misleading, incomplete or unverifiable can be disputed. If the credit bureau cannot verify that the information you are disputing is correct, then it must be deleted from your report. Credit repair services can help you with the process of disputing inaccurate or questionable items.

Q: How much do credit repair services cost?

A: It depends on the company you choose. Most will charge you a one-time set-up fee to review your credit situation. They will then decide whether or not they can help you, and if so, they will prepare a plan of action for cleaning up your credit and usually assign your account to one of their specialists. This fee varies widely among different companies, but is frequently less than $100. Most of them charge a monthly fee (usually $40 to $80 per month, although it may occasionally be more or less) to provide services like dispute assistance, credit monitoring, and credit education. Some even provide identity theft insurance.

Q: Can't I just repair my credit on my own?

A: You can, but it is a time-consuming and often frustrating process. One of the primary benefits of hiring credit repair services is that they save you time. For every item on your credit report that you want to dispute, you must write a letter, send it, monitor the time that has passed (credit agencies only have 30 days to respond), follow up with the bureau if the deadline has passed and so on. If you have a lot of incorrect or unverifiable information on your report, this process can take a substantial portion of time.

Conclusion

Millions of Americans have damaged credit, but with the help of credit repair services, bad credit can usually be improved significantly. The Fair Credit Reporting Act gives consumers the right to challenge incorrect information. Take advantage of that right and investigate your credit report today. A credit repair service can help you dispute incorrect information and save you a great deal of time. If you have bad credit, it's in your best interest to take advantage of the great things credit repair services can offer.

How Credit Repair Company Work

Credit Repair Companies, generally speaking, have gotten a "bad rap" and not without good reason! A lot of scammers have masqueraded as credit repair agencies, promising to help relieve their clients of their credit problems. But in the end, all they have "relieved" them of is their hard-earned money!

But not all credit repair organizations are crooks! There are many reputable credit repair companies that provide a valuable and much needed service to the consumer.

A poor credit score can dig deep into your pockets and drain away your hard-earned money on excessively high interest rates. At the same time, repairing your credit is a time-consuming process, which requires close follow-up and often specialized and customized appeals for removing inaccurate negative data from your credit report.

You are probably aware that there are a huge number of credit repair companies and credit repair lawyers ready to offer their services, but you don't know which one to choose. You may have heard too many stories of people being left with nothing to show for their money, and for that reason, you are very wary and indecisive.

Here are five factors that will help you reach an intelligent and informed decision:

1. Professionalism - is the company you are considering professional? Check out their web site carefully and see whether you are comfortable with what you find there.

- Is the website easily navigable?
- Does it have a page with FAQs that can help guide you?

- Do they have a live chat or fast-response email service to answer your queries?
- Is there counseling offered free by the companies?
- Does it make extraordinary claims? (NOT a good sign!)

Check carefully every aspect, and trust both your logic and your gut feelings.

2. Ethical - it is extremely important that the credit repair companies you choose behaves ethically. Do not fall for agencies that claim they can remove all your negative accounts, whether they are being accurately reported or not. You should expect to remove only those accounts which are being inaccurately reported.

Do not be tempted to avail of illegal means to increase your score. You might be inviting more trouble than you could handle. Check on the Internet for reviews or feedback on the credit repair companies you have chosen. Be on the lookout for any reports of scams. Check whether the company is affiliated with reputed organizations such as the ECRA (Ethical Credit Repair Alliance) or the BBB (Better Business Bureau) which will ensure that they adhere to strict codes of conduct.

3. 24/7 monitoring - credit repair means much more than just "credit repair." It means counseling, education, awareness, and monitoring among other things. Regular monitoring and immediate intervention when negative remarks find their way into your credit report are far more effective in maintaining a good credit score that just repairing it. Are the credit repair companies offering you more? Do they have these ancillary services on their menu?

4. Reasonable - it is true that credit repair companies are in business to turn a profit. However, this should not be at the cost of their clients. The best business relationships, ones that survives time and changes in technology, are often

associated with the offer of value-for-money by companies. You need to feel happy about the price and services offered. Research these aspects well enough so that you will be empowered to bargain for the best offer. Do not feel shy about negotiating.

5. Offer solutions - you need solutions. The best credit repair companies are those who are able to draw you out and learn about your problems in detail, so that they can work out a customized solution for you as an individual. This is very important because no two financial problems will be alike, and what works fine for one person might not work at all for another. Look for a credit repair agency that is geared toward offering solutions - "tailor made" solutions for YOU!

Many of us hear the term "credit repair services" and automatically think it's a scam. This is because many of them are, and only attempt to steal your money and drip-dry your wallet. However, we'll be taking a look at what an ideal, reputable, efficient, and proven credit Repair Company does. This company assists people in repairing their credit quickly, usually within a couple months. This can take at least a year for a novice to try to do, if they are successful. The most important factor to keep in mind when seeking credit repair services is that it is a marathon, not a sprint. It takes delicate time and resources to repair a credit report, so you need to find a company that is passionate about helping you, and has a proven track record. We will also discuss tips and tricks you can use to ensure you're picking a winning company to help keep yourself and your wallet safe.

Firstly, let's go over safety. This is the main concern when selecting a credit repair company. A good credit repair company doesn't have the words "wire" or anything of the sorts on their site. They proudly accept payment via check, credit, or debit card, just as any legitimate business does. You won't be sending nonrefundable money to them, or making cash deposits into their account. These are the same trusted payment options you use everywhere else, and credit cards are also backed by the credit companies' award winning fraud protection, so you know you're safe. Other companies that claim to want to truly help you, often drip-feed your wallet taking $100 month-by-month, and falling back on the excuse that they never promised anything, but would "try" to do their best for you. As much as it's a fact that nothing can be promised, because ultimately it's up to the credit bureaus, they live on that excuse to suck peoples' wallets dry. A good credit repair company isn't like that, and you're welcome to ask any of their many satisfied customers.

Second, some type of reasoning behind their services is what you're looking for. How can they help you? What are they capable of clearing from your reports? What is the turnaround time? Do they have any examples of their work? These are all great questions to be asking not only the company, but also yourself when sourcing professional credit repair help. A good company separates itself from the fakes out there in a number of ways. They show you a detailed in-depth video of a consumer's credit report. A video would be ideal so you can then note the differences. They go over how their report looked at one point, and also at another point to show the improvements. You want to see a timeframe of around a couple months. They should take time to show you the basics of what they can do for you in order to begin building trust with potential clients.

By now, you're hopefully leaning towards using a good credit repair company for your credit report issues. But how do they work? A good credit repair company works off of government legislature to fairly represent you to the credit reporting bureaus. To ease some of your curiosity, their strategy involves them using, on your behalf, the Fair Credit Billing Act, Fair Credit Reporting Act, and the Fair Debt

Collection Practices Act. True knowledge and understanding of all these pieces of legislation gives us the ability and the confidence to legally challenge items in your credit reports. Each one of these acts can be viewed at: www.ftc.gov. You may also be asking how long it takes to see results. Once you receive your credit reports from all 3 credit bureaus, a good credit repair company will aggressively remove the negative debt from your credit report. By law, the credit agencies must respond to your dispute letters within 30 days from the actual dispute claim, and you should definitely see results on your credit file within 30-45 days.

Hopefully, the above paragraph gave you a reasonable idea as to how they operate. They're basically like your lawyers, but to the credit bureaus! Trust them to work with you, and you surely won't be disappointed. If you have any questions, comments, or concerns, reach out! The first step to bettering your financial future is to allow them to help you in combating the intimidating credit bureaus. You could also try to fix your credit report yourself, but when a novice attempts to do that, the credit bureaus log each and every dispute, so this can make it harder later on down the line when you attempt to seek professional help. Let the expert's help you from the get go! It is important that you don't begin contacting the credit bureaus and seeking disputes without knowing what you're doing. This can only hurt you and make you look less serious to them, and they will attempt to take advantage of that. You must convey to them that you mean business, and allowing a professional outfit to represent you is generally the best option available.

So why hire a professional outfit to professionally represent you? It has gotten to the point where almost everything is based on your credit history. With a better and more accurate credit file, you can receive lower credit card and home mortgage interest rates, lower automobile finance charges, lower down payments, lower insurance rates, and more pre-approved credit. Foremost, restoring your credit will give you more peace of mind and will also eliminate certain stress. Therefore you can benefit greatly by taking advantage of professional services. Most of the important things in your life such as your car, job, financial standing, and job, can all be affected by how well your credit report is. If you are in the position where you need credit repair assistance, you need to consult a professional company that specializes in removing derogatory remarks on your accounts, remove accounts that are in collections, and other bad histories within your credit report that can prevent you from obtaining future loans, having to satisfy for higher interest rates, and other obstacles throughout your financial future. You may also want to fix your credit fast in case you need to acquire any new loans for a family emergency, a new vehicle, getting a new job, or even a new home.

Why Credit Repair Companies Are Necessary

Credit has been essential to every person's purchasing capacity. With all the available products you wish to possess, you cannot afford to buy them all. That is the power of credit, making things possible for you. That is why having a good credit is really important. Having a good credit rating means having more opportunities to purchase. And knowing that there are many credit cards available today, all you need is to have a good credit record. The better the credit, the more options can be offered to these people. But the truth is, having a good credit rating is hard to achieve. Especially with many different cards one can maintain, it will be hard for a person to resist the temptation of buying more.

For this reason, we really are in need of credit repair. If you are one of the many people who are in dire need for credit repair, do not worry any longer. There are numerous credit repair companies and they are even available online. Just that is just easy! These services can really help you out. The problem now is deciding what repair service you should choose. However, choosing what repair service depends on how bad your rating is.

For people who really have a large amount of debt, they need specific online credit repair services. You can avail of credit counseling so that you will be guided on what to do with your situation. These credit repair services can help in a few different ways. The first step these credit repair companies do is to work with you and ensure accurate credit report from you. It must be made sure that you always pay attention on your credit rating. This is a very common problem since most creditors do not speak of the real situation. Inaccuracies happen most of the time that is why it is very important to deal with them immediately to prevent more damages on your record. Using secured credit cards with a debt consolidation loan can give valuable insight to help you recover from the pit that you unfortunately fell in. So, the earlier you help yourself, the more chances of faster recovery from a bad credit.

If you can not afford to pay immediately, these companies will just take care of your credit card balance. In worst cases, they will tell their clients to claim bankruptcy. Credit repair companies have saved a large majority of people who suffer from bad credit. If you have bad credit, then search for the best repair service now. It is not too late. You can still do something.

How to Find The Particular Best Credit Repair Company

Some people would actually prefer to work with a credit repair company when compared with go throughout the trouble regarding fixing their credit problems on their own. But exactly how will you know if the company an individual hired is the best credit repair company?

Getting impressed using two or more companies is just typical since most of them give quite tempting purports to their customers. The one line which separates each and every company is the actual intense truthfulness on their claims. And a lot of the time, you might be already around the trap when you find out that you have just vacant promises, poor service that produces low quality results and dishonest practices. How can you tell the sincere offer from the tricking ones? The best credit company will probably be hired using the assistance of the following advice.

Best Credit Repair Company tip #1: Very best Customer Service. Sometimes you should be patient adequate to support your self when controlling the bureaus. Consumers would really welcome someone who could lend them a hand within times when their particular credit isn't on their healthiest level. How well the client service associates answer each of the customer's inquiries is amongst the bases regarding finding the best credit repair business.

Best Credit Repair Company tip #2: Best Track Record. The company overview must be good enough as well as real to impress the customers. Inspect how a company was established and the way long it was in the business. Lawsuits as well as court incidents are parts of the public information so you are able to check if the company is associated with any before. A word of caution on depending on a Better Business Bureau rating; it has ended up discovered that numerous A-rated companies, whom had much more complaints than C rated companies, obtained the higher score because they paid out the Better business bureau big bucks for it. This makes your rating associated with credit businesses to be difficult to rely on.

Best Credit Repair Company idea #3: Fair Company warranty and Cancellations Policy. And they're willing to reimbursement your repayment if ever you are not satisfied with the service these people rendered.

The actual best credit repair company now offers to check the advancement of your credit rating online. Everything that offers something to do with your current interest is installed in the open. Whether you want to monitor your concern or not, they'll provide you the info since that is part of the services they offer.

Here are several of the most picked out services offered by the best credit repair firm:

- Assist with creditors, at the appropriate interval, by mailing Creditor Direct letters
- Send out dispute queries

- Ask for the office to change or even delete any inaccurate info found on the report
- Guide you as you deal with the actual fraudulent activities of a number of collection agencies.
- Guide you in creating your very good image throughout the eyes in the bureaus and also lenders
- Solve your identity theft problem

Truthful along with realistic include the two qualities that best credit repair organization are. The best credit repair business wouldn't promise a person things that will never happen in reality; instead they are going to give you the time where final results can really take place. One cannot compare the length of time they notice progress around the service they acquired via another consumer since enhancement varies on each circumstance.

Should I Hire a Credit Repair Company to Repair My Credit Or Should I Do it Myself?

Should I hire a credit repair company? This is by far one of the most widely asked questions by people who need to fix their credit and get their FICO scores increase. The answer however is not that cut and dry, while some people should hire a company to get the job done most should not and you will find out why in the article below!

Why You Do Not Need a Credit Repair Company

The biggest reason you do not need to hire a company to fix your credit is the simple fact that you can get the exact same results for a lot less money, often a lot faster as well! This is a fact that not many people realize!

First you must understand that these for profit companies are in business for one reason, to make money. They make that money by charging clients a monthly fee. So the longer they can charge you that fee the more they make giving them incentive to take longer then needed!

In most cases, you pay them a $75 set up fee then on average $99 a month.So just doing some basic math shows that for 3 months of credit repair you will be paying $372! Plus what these companies will not tell you is that all letters and correspondence from the bureaus will be sent to you and you will have to mail, or drive it down to them, so it is not really a hands off process for you!

If I Do Not Hire a Company To Fix My FICO Score What Should I Do?

The best way to get your FICO scores increased and your credit report cleaned up is to use a credit repair kit. However not just any of these kits will do, you need to make sure that you buy a the right kit that is going to supply you everything you need to get to work!

What Does a Good Credit Repair Kit Contain?

- A Step By Step Plan To Follow
- Credit Dispute Letter Templates
- A Plan To Rebuild Your Credit History
- Tips To Manage and Pay Down Your Current Debt Levels
- Tips on How To Deal With Creditors
- Bonus Products To Help Yo Get The Most From Your Efforts
- How To Order and Read Your Credit Report

Choose the Best Credit Repair Service for You

When you are looking to hire a company to fix your credit you should know what your goals are. This should be researched just like any other professional that we need and use. I will cover the five areas you want to compare when picking the best credit repair company.

The first thing you want to know is what you are getting with the company. There are many companies out there that simply mail out template dispute letters to the credit bureaus alone. These types of credit repair companies often get you what we refer to as soft deletions. Soft deletions are items which are taken off your credit report in the verification process but end back on your report often in a matter of weeks.

You want a company who disputes with the credit bureaus but who also goes to the source of the problems. The source will be your creditors and collection companies, removing items from the source to ensure they do not just pop back on your report. Correcting the problem at the source will insure that the credit correction is permanent.

Total cost is almost always overlooked by the consumer who is lured in by small monthly payments. The part that they fail to mention is the end date;because it does not exist. Yes the monthly payment may seem appealing at first but when you compare, they often cost more than $1,000 a year. Consumers can also be stuck in this never-ending billing for years with little to no results.

A recent study showed that with only a 50 point increase to their credit score the average consumer would save $400 a month. Now do the total cost on that same low monthly payment service for two years. With a price of $1000 per year, now add in the 24 months of lost savings at $400 a month. The total cost would really be $11,600, scary but true! You always want to choose a credit repair service built for speed, a service that will go after all negative inaccurate information immediately and then on every single round.

The time line in which you can expect your results is a big factor as exposed in the total cost. It has been my experience that when people are looking for credit repair there is generally a major purchase happening or coming soon. The time that you will get your results should be explained but if any service guarantees a specific outcome in an exact time they are violating the law. Find out what the average client has experienced for the success you need to achieve.

Results are the foundation to better credit. If you do not get results then you are just wasting your hard-earned money. When choosing a company you want to see actual results. Any company who is successful should be able to produce real results for you. The real results you want to see are actual credit reports showing the before and after results including the actual responses from the credit bureaus themselves. Client testimonials are also a great resource to explore the best are in video with real people explaining in their own words of what a service has done to help them.

The reputation that a company has can say a lot about their product or service. Credit repair has earned a well deserved black eye because of the deceptive practices of the unethical companies out there. The internet provides you the ability to quickly research the company that you are considering hiring. If they have a bad online reputation, come up on one of the many consumer protection sites, or you cannot find them period you better be very careful.

The Growth Of The Credit Repair Business Opportunity

Everyone is saying that times are hard and that no one is making any money nowadays. But that doesn't mean you have to believe it. Rise above all the negativity about who is earning what (and who isn't earning anything) and do something for yourself. Start a business that has proven to be successful with your own credit repair business.

Why should you start a credit repair business?

Even if you have just recently started looking into what business to start, you probably already realize the advantages of a credit repair business! There are many reasons to consider credit repair.

It is a business that can be run easily at home, with little start up cost required. You can do it from your kitchen table with just your laptop. You can do it as a full-time job or just for a couple of hours each day, and you get to set your own hours. And, it is a business that can succeed even if the economy is bad.

But many people love being in the credit repair business because it gives them the chance to help people while earning a living. Credit repair may not be the first thing that comes to mind when you are thinking of ways to help people, but it really is!

When a client has a bad credit rating, they may not be able to get the new car they need, or the home of their dreams. Bad credit may mean they can't start a business, or even get a job.

Even worse (and more frustrating), is that sometimes having a bad credit rating isn't even the client's fault! Mistakes can easily happen on a person's credit report; their name or social security number can be mixed up with someone else's.

These errors can be very difficult to correct, and problems from these errors can get even more serious. Your client may not only have problems getting the loan they need for a new car, but they may be getting harassing phone calls from creditors. And, they may end up having their wages garnished. All for something that isn't their fault!

Or maybe your client didn't take their credit very seriously in their younger days, and now they need some help getting their credit report cleaned up. They are anxious to make things right, but they just need a little help figuring out the best way to repair their credit.

This is where you come in as a credit repair professional, where you get to be the hero!

The FTC and members of congress realize credit report errors are a problem

Even the government is concerned about credit report errors and the impact these can have on consumers. According to a Federal Trade Commission (FTC) study of the U.S. credit reporting industry, 5% of consumers had errors on one of their three major credit reports. These errors could lead to them paying more for important things such as auto loans and insurance.

The study also found that:

- One in four consumers identified errors on their credit reports that might affect their credit scores
- One in five consumers had an error that was corrected by a credit reporting agency after it was disputed, on at least one of their three credit reports
- Four out of five consumers who filed disputes experienced some modification to their credit report
- Slightly more than one in 10 consumers saw a change in their credit score after the credit reporting agency modified errors on their credit report
- Approximately one in 20 consumers had a maximum score change of more than 25 points and only one in 250 consumers had a maximum score change of more than 100 points.

Sen. Claire McCaskill (D-Mo.) testified in front of a Senate Commerce Committee at a hearing on inaccurate information on credit reports. She told them, "Errors can mean the difference between obtaining a car loan or not, or paying a higher price for a mortgage. Errors can result in credit issuers, like a small town bank, declining credit to a potentially valuable customer, or issuing credit to a riskier customer than intended."

She suggested that the industry needed financial penalties to keep similar mistakes from happening. Sen. David Rockefeller (D-WV), chairman of the Senate Commerce Committee, also suggested that legislation was needed.

"The credit bureaus have a legal obligation to take all reasonable steps to maximize the possible accuracy of credit reports, and when they do contain errors, provide consumers with the means to fix them," said Rockefeller. "I expect this industry to do everything it can to ensure that the system works for the ones that it impacts the most, everyday Americans. If today's hearing uncovers problems with the credit reporting industry, I urge these companies to tackle those problems with a sense of urgency."

Clearly, consumers need help with this important issue.

How to take advantage of a credit repair business opportunity

The first step to helping your clients, once you decide to be a part of the credit repair business, is to learn all you can about the credit repair business. You need to learn the secrets to credit repair and how to submit credit disputes on behalf of your clients. You need to have a thorough understanding of how credit reports work, so you can help your clients to understand them.

It may sound like too much to take on, especially if you don't consider yourself a financial wizard. However, there are some simple ways that you can get credit repair business training.

- To start with, you can read as much about credit and credit repair as you can. Look around online for credit repair forums and join in on the discussions.
- Get your own credit report and take a close look at it.
- Find a mentor, and someone who has been in the credit repair business for years.

This may not be as easy as it sounds, though. This is where a credit repair business training resource comes in. This is a great way to communicate with professionals who have been in the industry for years. It will also help you to educate yourself about the industry and the best way you can help your clients. It will help you understand what you can and can't do when negotiating with your client's creditors and collection agencies, and it will help you to ensure that your client won't be taken advantage of.

Chapter Three

Credit Repair Scams and How to Avoid Them

Recently my friends at Liberty Mortgage Company sent me an email alert regarding the latest scams in the credit repair market. The mortgage company receives applications every day that have some credit issues that could block the path to home ownership. Many of the people they talk with think that their credit issues are being repaired. Unfortunately, these applicants often have fallen for one of the many credit repair scams that set their traps for well meaning home buyers with a few credit problems.

Mortgage loan qualification requirements are stricter today than in the past - FHA / VA and Conventional Home Loan sources are requiring ever higher FICO scores so the average applicant may need to improve their credit report before they can qualify for a home loan. With the demand for housing beginning to grow, it makes a very ripe market for scammers. Most popular credit repair scams promise to wipe your credit report clean of all negative information. They usually charge an up front fee, sometimes as much as $1,500 for their service. Often all the scammers will do is dispute all the negative information on your credit report. This is something you can do on your own for free.

Another "We will fix it" scam for a fee is to tell you that they will get you a new social security number. The idea is with a new number most credit agencies would have to start a new file under that number with your name and it wouldn't have the negative information that may have been reported under your old SS number. The truth is, the Social Security Administration almost never agrees to assign a new SS number to an individual who already has a file and number. What these "credit repair" scammers are doing is filing with the IRS for an EIN (Employer

Identification Number) under your name. It's also a nine-digit number that looks like a social security number, but is actually a number assigned to a business. This number is used by the IRS to identify companies for tax payment purposes.

If you fall for this one, the consequences are far reaching. By using an EIN as your SS number, you change how your income is reported to the IRS. You'll find it's a big problem when you retire and the Social Security Administration has no record of your work history. Not only will your social security checks be in jeopardy, you may find yourself accused of conspiring to commit fraud with possible jail time in your future. Remember, there is no magic formula to repairing your credit score, and no big secrets that only a credit repair company has access to. Credit score repair is actually a fairly simple process of writing letters and then following up, and it can be done by anyone. The scammers are out there, and they want your money so be informed and don't be a victim.

The Solution to Post-Bankruptcy Bad Credit

Doing credit repair after you have had a bankruptcy is probably one of the smartest things you can do for your credit profile. If you believed the story your attorney told you after your bankruptcy that your credit report would take care of itself, you are probably regretting that. No doubt your credit report does not look like you hoped it would after your bankruptcy.

Self credit repair is your solution. Don't be misled by credit repair companies that claim they can get your bankruptcy removed from your report. The fact of the matter is that when you fill out a loan application you will most likely have to declare if you have had a bankruptcy within the last 7 years anyhow. If you don't disclose this, you are committing fraud. You should not commit fraud! It is dangerous.

So, your bankruptcy is discharged and your credit report still looks like a mess. You still have accounts that show up with balances on them when they were included in your bankruptcy and should show no balance. Other accounts show a balance of zero, but they still have a negative rating on them. You are probably in a situation where you pretty much need to dispute anything that is negative on your credit report. You have the right to dispute anything you don't feel is reporting 100% accurately because you have the right to have everything on your report be 100% accurate. That is the law found in the Fair Credit Reporting Act.

You should already have a copy of your credit report. You can get this online or you can probably get it from the lender that denied your credit. Just ask them for it. They can usually scan it and email it to you as a PDF file. Once you have your report, read it and decide what you think you need to dispute. This can be a bit of a daunting task, especially if you don't really know how to read the report. If you got your report from you loan officer, call them and ask them to help you decipher the report. You might even be able to get them to put an 'X' next to anything on your report that they think is hurting your profile. Since you don't want to dispute anything that is helping your profile, this will give you a good place to start deciding what you are going to dispute in your Credit Repair letters. You can dispute collections, charge offs, public records, bad debts. As I stated previously, if you have had a bankruptcy, you probably have a lot of accounts on your report that still show balances when they should not since they were included in your bankruptcy. Start with these.

Now that you know what you want to dispute, you need to write credit dispute letters. This is basically what a credit repair company would do for you, but you can do it on your own pretty easily. There is software available on the web that you can purchase and there are free sites that you can use. You should seek these out if you would like to save yourself a lot of time. If you have a lot of time on your hands (who does?) you can write the credit repair letters out yourself.

Sending out basic credit dispute letters is typically very effective, especially if the letters really look like they are from you and not created by a program. Some software will actually help you do that. You don't want the text and font to be the same on all the letters. Change it up a bit.

From personal experience helping people send out basic credit dispute letters, I can attest that they can be very effective in getting your report to be more accurate, and in improving your credit score tremendously.

What Everyone With Bad Credit Should Know About Credit Repair Services

If you're one of the millions of people in America with bad or damaged credit, don't despair. There are several things you can do to improve your credit. If you're looking for information about how to repair your credit and credit repair services, you've come to the right place. In this article we'll discuss the definition of bad credit and the benefits of using credit repair services. By the end of this article you should be able to start repairing your credit today, whether you choose to do so on your own, or hire a professional service to assist you.

What is Considered Bad Credit?

Most lenders define bad credit as any credit score lower than 620. After the subprime mortgage fiasco, some lenders are even raising that bar to 640. In addition to your payment patterns and amount of outstanding debt, your time on the job and your time living at your current address make up a portion of your creditworthiness. People who stay at the same employer and residence longer are considered more creditworthy than those who change jobs or move frequently.

If you are interested in improving your credit, it's in your best interest to know what your credit score is, even if you are afraid to find out! Order a copy of your credit report and make sure you get reports from all three major credit reporting agencies: Equifax, Experian and Transunion. Some lenders use the top score and some use a blended score so it is important to know what is on each report. Once you know where you stand you can begin the process of repairing your credit.

Benefits of Credit Repair Services

Credit repair services can help in a number of ways. Many of them offer packages that include obtaining your credit report, looking for inaccuracies and contacting the reporting agencies on your behalf. The primary benefit of credit repair services is that they save you time and effort. Most of what a credit repair service can do, you can do for yourself. But just like many services, the benefit is in convenience and saving time. It's akin to repairing your own car; it is technically possible for you to do it yourself, but if you lack knowledge and experience in repairing cars, you could probably save a lot of time and frustration by paying someone else to do it for you.

There are credit repair service companies that do not offer a true value because they use ineffective and/or outdated tactics. Some of the large and well-known companies are guilty of this. Make sure you investigate the credit repair service that you're considering and find out exactly what they offer. Get all of their claims in writing and find out what their refund policy is. Do not pay any fees up front (with the exception of a one-time set-up fee), and when in doubt, walk away.

Credit problems can be difficult to deal with, but help is available. The first step is determining your credit score and looking at the contents of your credit reports. Then decide if you want to take on the task of disputing negative listings yourself, or if you want to bring in a professional credit repair service to help. Credit repair services can save you time and effort although they can't really do anything for you that you couldn't do for yourself. When shopping for a credit repair service, make sure you investigate them thoroughly to protect yourself from any scams. With the information in this article you should be better informed about the best way to repair your credit.

Improve Your Credit Score - Credit Repair Companies Put To The Test

As a consumer credit advocate, I get asked all the time can credit repair companies improve your credit score?

The simple fact is yes! You can improve your credit score and get pre-approved for credit cards and prime rate loans by hiring a reputable credit repair company to work as your advocate. There are many companies that advertise credit repair services, but asking the right questions will help you decide which company is the most reputable and the best fit for your goals. With the best credit repair company on your side, collecting the facts will help you improve your credit score.

In order to improve your credit score, I suggest you ask the following questions before hiring a credit repair company:

• Do they have a Better Business Bureau record? Legitimate and reputable companies maintain a satisfactory record with the Better Business Bureau (BBB). Accredited businesses are committed to its customers and maintain the highest standards of trust and reliability. Visit bbb.org to verify satisfactory rankings of the credit repair companies you are considering.

• Is the company a law firm? Attorneys are bound by rules of ethics that require them to act with absolute integrity. Attorneys are responsible for looking after their clients' best interest and are required to utilize custom approaches to call upon every means possible to obtain positive results for their clients. Most companies, law firms or not, charge around $39 per month, so you should demand representation from a law firm for the same price to improve your credit score.

• Is a free consultation available? You should be able to discuss your goals and expectations before you enter into a contract with any credit repair company. You should also be advised of your rights under The Fair Credit Reporting Act (FCRA) [http://www.825credit.com/fcra.html] and learn how the law is on your side to help you improve your credit score.

• Can you cancel at anytime? Hiring the right credit repair company to represent you can help you gain better credit and improve your credit score. As results are obtained, you will not require the services of a credit repair company forever. Once you improve your credit score, reputable credit repair companies will allow you to cancel your account.

• Are online account management tools available? Reputable credit repair companies allow you, the client, to choose how you want your case managed to improve your credit score. Good credit repair law firms will give you options and advice on how to achieve the best results and will allow you to manage your case via a secure online client website.

• How many items have they removed for their clients? Legitimate credit repair companies have a proven track record of success. Companies such as Lexington

Law have helped over 400,000 clients delete millions of items that are serious enough to harm your access to credit, prime loan rates and even a job.

I understand the challenges that you've encountered on your quest for better credit and, more importantly, a better life. You've been climbing a mountain; the right credit repair company can help you reach the top.

Fixing Your Finances With Credit Repair

If you do not think credit repair can help you out there are some things you need to consider. First of all how did you get into financial trouble? Did you lose your job? Did the monthly expenses overtake the monthly income? Did you make some bad investments? Whatever the reason there is something you can do to help and this rebuild. It will not be fun, it will not be easy, it will not be quick, but you do have to do it. If you are in financial trouble because you lost your job or you still have it but are trying to find a new one with no luck there may be something working against you. Let's say you find a job that pays well, has great benefits, and it fits everything you want. Well there are probably at least one hundred people who would be in the same situation as you are and they want that job too. Now if you all have similar qualifications; college degree, years of experience and so on, what is to separate you from the other one? More important, what will make you stick out when they are looking at you as an employee?

Shockingly the answer is your credit score. Many companies, in fact over forty percent of the companies around the country, have been using a credit check as part of their application process for years. This has been going on for decades and companies use it to thin the list of qualified applicants. It mainly happens with jobs that have certain financial responsibilities but that can cover so many jobs these days. Even companies feel it is a bit unfair but they cannot find another way to fairly choose between qualified applicants. So this becomes the most common method to help them make a decision and if you have been struggling with bills lately, you are going to be in trouble.

There are other things that can be hurt if you have a low score. Your ability to get loans, financing options and the interest you will have to pay when you borrow money. It really seems unfair that because your number is low you have to pay more a month on money owed. However, there is something you can do about it. Fixing your score with traditional methods takes too long to help you save money now. The only way to really save money is if you use credit repair now. By using the methods of credit repair to fix your score you will be able to reduce monthly payments with loan and credit companies. If they do not agree to adjust the deal and you have a good score you can transfer to another lender who will be happy to take you.

Section 609 Credit Repair Method

To understand how the FCRA Section 609 credit repair method works, it is important to understand that the FCRA was written before the advent of the internet. As such, they require the credit reporting agencies to have physical copies of all documentation to support each account that is being reported on. This is a problem for these agencies as virtually all credit items added to your credit report these days are submitted electronically. This in turn, means that it is rare for any documents to be reviewed prior to changes being made to your credit report.

Essentially, the credit reporting agencies just give all creditors the benefit of the doubt when new information IS added to your file. You can use this to your advantage by asking for hard-copy verification via Section 609 of the FCRA for virtually anything negative that is listed on your credit report. You simply need to use the following letter and not be deterred by any scare tactics that the credit reporting agencies will use to cover their tracks as they will try everything in their power to avoid having to tell you that they do n't have the physical documentation.

There are many sections and subsections in the Fair Credit Reporting Act that was established in 1971. Remember that the FCRA was established to protect the consumer from unfair lending and collections practices. One such section that can help the consumer dispute debt and information contained in their credit report is Section 609.

How does Section 609 help you repair your credit?

Section 609 of the Fair Credit Reporting Act says that upon a consumer's request, the credit reporting agency must be able to provide certain information to the consumer.

What this means is that you legally have options to get the credit reporting agencies to verify the debt on your account. I went into an explanation of the verification of debt in the last blog post so you should understand it a little bit. Like we talked about, a lot of the information on your credit report may be inaccurate.

Some of it may be accurate. It's important to make sure that the debt on your credit report and all the information contained therein is accurate. The credit reporting agency must be able to prove that the account listed belongs to you, and also where they received this information regarding this account.

The legal wording in Section 609 of the FCRA doesn't have information pertaining to whether the negative account is valid or not. What the law does care about is that the information the credit reporting agencies have on you and the accounts listed in your report is enough to provide proper verification under the law.

When you send a verification letter to the agencies, you are sending a request under Section 609 of the FCRA. You will be asking that the credit reporting agencies follow the law and verify the debt as requested. The credit reporting agencies have 30 days from receiving this letter to go through the verification process and get back to you.Make sure you keep foolproof records of everything you do through this process.

When you mail the 609 letters to the credit reporting agencies, send them certified mail with return receipt. This will cost you a little bit of money on the front end, but it will be worth it to have peace of mind in your record keeping. When mailing them certified, you will be able to track them and see when they are received. If the credit reporting agency does not respond to your dispute request within 30 days of that date, they are in violation of the law and you can call them out on it.

If they fail to respond to your 609 letters within 30 days, you can request that the credit reporting agency removes the disputed items from your credit report since they neglected to follow the law.

Your letter may be classified as "frivolous" by the credit reporting agency. The reason this happens is that they use computers to scan the incoming letters and classify them into categories. It would be rare for an incoming letter to go directly into a human's hands first thing. The credit reporting agency will then respond to your inquiry letting you know that it thinks your request is frivolous. You will have to send a second round of 609 letters.

To avoid having to do this process multiple times, you can put it a little more work on the front end, ensuring that a human will handle your dispute request instead of a computer.

When making the 609 letters to send to the credit reporting agencies, do not use an internet form letter. I will later give you examples of letters you can send but do not use them word for word. Instead, use them as a template or a guideline for what you will send.

Also, do not type your letter up in a word processing program like Microsoft Word or Google Docs. Instead, write your letter out by hand. Use blue ink, since it is harder for the computers to decipher. Write in print rather than cursive, as we want the human that looks over your information to be able to clearly read what you are asking of them. It is also a good idea to get the letters notarized before you mail them. This will prove to the credit companies that you are who you say you are.

Responses

When the credit reporting agency responds to your dispute request, they will do so by mail. There are a few different ways they can respond.

One way is a full and complete verification of your debt, like a copy of the original dated contract bearing your signature. If this is the response you get, the debt has legally been verified and you will be hard pressed to get them to remove it from your report.

Another way they try to verify the debt is not a true verification at all. The credit reporting agency may send you a copy of a statement on the line of credit that they received as proof from the original furnisher of the loan, or from a collection agency collecting the debt for the original lender. This is not solid proof of your debt. You will need to send another letter, requesting to see the copy of the original dated contract that has your signature on it.

The ideal outcome is that they credit reporting agency has no way to verify the debt in compliance with the law, and when they respond to you they tell you that. If this is the response, they need to delete the credit line off of your credit report. When the negative information is deleted, your credit score will improve.

After Dispute, Is it Gone for Good?

This is where some people get hung up. You are disputing your credit lines with the credit reporting agencies, usually not the person or company reporting the information to the agency. Unfortunately, sometimes even if the credit reporting agency deletes the inaccurate information from your credit report, it can come back to haunt you. If the original furnisher of the debt sees that the information has been knocked off, they may try to get it reinstated. They could also sell it to a collections agency which would start the process of verification and 609 letters all over.

If your debt was already with a collections agency when you disputed it and had it removed from your credit report, they won't be happy either. They could also try to get it put back on your report, or they might even sell it to yet another collections agency. Once again, this would restart the whole process of verification/609 letters.

Another thing you need to understand is that just because the debt is no longer reported on your credit report, that does not mean you no longer owe it if it is a valid debt. Make note of the fact that I said valid debt. If the information concerning the debt is invalid and you can prove it, you should have nothing to worry about during the dispute process.

However, if the debt is valid and you are just trying to get the negative reporting on the debt removed from your credit report; this process does not absolve you from paying that debt.

The 609 letters you sent to the credit reporting agencies were not sent to dispute whether the debt is valid or not. The purpose of the 609 letters you sent was to force the credit reporting agency's hand into proving to you that they have the legal right to report the disputed debt. If the credit reporting agency is unable to provide you with physical proof of the verification of the debt, they cannot report it on your credit report as they have no way to prove it is 100 percent accurate. The FCRA demands that the credit reporting agencies ensure that everything reported by them is factual, and this is where you have them most of the time.

Again, I will say if the debt actually belongs to you and the only reason you are disputing it is that of negative reporting, you still owe the debt. If you do not pay up on the debt, it will soon be sold to a collections agency, and then guess what? You will be right back in this situation again. Requesting that the credit reporting agencies verify that the information being reported by the collections agency is correct. If you are not careful and do not pay! attention, this an quickly turn into a vicious repeating cycle.

With the following "609 letters", you will need to be sure to always include a copy of a photo identification as well as a copy of your social security card (also include your past residences for 5 years). This is due to the fact that the FCRA only requires the credit reporting agencies to respond to individuals in writing if they provide these details. Without it, your letters will simply be ignored. When disputing accounts, it is also important to never dispute more than 22 at one time. This is the magic number, anything more than that will cause you dispute to be considered frivolous. Additionally, you will want to ensure you hand label your envelopes as type envelopes will be opened far less often.

Section 609 Dispute Letter Template

Name

Address

(Credit Bureau Name)

Date

To Whom It May Concern:

This letter is a formal complaint that you are reporting inaccurate and incomplete credit information. I am distressed that you have included the below information in my credit profile and have failed to maintain reasonable procedures in your operations to assure maximum possible accuracy in the credit reports you publish.

Credit reporting laws ensure that bureaus report only 100% accurate credit information. Every step must be taken to assure the information reported is completely accurate and correct. The following information therefore needs to be re-investigated. I respectfully request to be provided proof that these inquiries were in fact authorized With an instrument bearing my signature, and for legitimate business purposes. Failing that the unauthorized inquiry must be deleted from the report as soon as possible:

(Accounts you wish to have removed from your report)

Please delete this misleading information, and supply a corrected credit profile to all creditors who have received a copy within the last 6 months or the last 2 years for employment purposes.

Additionally, please provide the name, address, and telephone number of each credit grantor or other subscriber.

Under federal law, you have 30 days to complete your re- investigation. Be advised that the description of the procedure used to determine the accuracy and completeness of the information is hereby requested as well, to be provided within 15 days of the completion of your re-investigation.

Sincerely,

(Signature)

Name

SSN#

I will be providing you with templates for the letters we discussed previously. In case you skipped over those blog post to get to the good stuff, I will give a brief explanation again here.

You can send a Section 609/Method of Verification Letter forcing the credit reporting agencies to verify that they have proof of your debt from the original lender.

You can send a goodwill letter, asking for compassion regarding late or missed payments on a line of credit.

You can send a letter asking a creditor for a Pay-to-Delete deal to remove information from your credit report.

You can send an HIPAA letter for information regarding healthcare accounts on your credit report.

Remember, do not copy these letters word for word. They are just templates to give you an idea as to how to word your letters that you send. Do not print these, instead, write them out by hand. Consider having them notarized to further prove your identity to the credit reporting agency. Send the letters by certified mail only, with a read receipt.

Along with the dispute letters, you will need to send information proving who you are. Write another document and include the following information:

Your full name. This includes your middle initial and any suffix such a Junior or III

The date you were born

Social Security Number (if you have one)

Current and former addresses from the past 5 years

A copy of a government-issued photo identification, such as a driver's license

Copy of bank statement, utility bill, insurance statement, etc. to verify your current address and identity

Sample Letter 1

[Date]

Credit Reporting Agency/Bureau

City, State, Zip

To Whom It May Concern:

I have reviewed a copy of my credit report and am writing to dispute some information that needs to be deleted from the report. These items should be deleted for the following reasons:

Item #

Reason for Deletion

According to the provisions for consumers provided in the Fair Credit Reporting Act 611(a) [15 USC 168ii(a)], these items I am disputing must be re-investigated or deleted from my credit record within 30 days. While the investigation is ongoing, these disputed items must be removed from reporting on my credit report, or listed as "in dispute". I am also requesting the contact information of the individuals you communicated with during your investigation into this dispute.

When the investigation is complete, please notify me that the above items have been deleted in accordance with 611 (a)(6) [15 USC (a) (6)]. Please also furnish me with an updated copy of my credit report, to be sent to the address below. According to 612 [15 USC 168ij], I should pay nothing for this report.

 If you need additional information or have any questions regarding this dispute, please contact me at address noted below.

Thank you.

Sincerely,

YOUR NAME

Address

City, State, Zip

Social Security #

Using Section 609 of the **FCRA** to Restore **NOT** Repair Credit

A simple, relatively unknown but proven legal strategy can be implemented to raise FICO scores 60 to 120 points. In 1999, H. Bruce McInnis Jr. in Maine looked at Section 609 of the Fair Credit Reporting Act (FCRA) and noticed something that, to his knowledge, nobody had ever noticed before; 609(c) (2) (E): "A consumer reporting agency is not required to remove accurate derogatory information from a consumer's file, unless the information is outdated under section 605 or cannot be verified."

If accurate derogatory information in the consumer's file cannot be verified, the reporting agency is required to remove it. This law requires every company that reports credit events, not just the original creditor companies, to be able to produce verifiable proof of the negative event. It holds the credit reporting agencies accountable for the negative information they pass on. This is obviously related to the right of debtors to challenge the accuracy of negative events reported on them. The intent of the government was to protect debtors from having inaccurate information used against them. The burden of proof is not entirely on the original creditors. All parties reporting this data are responsible for its accuracy. The companies that report credit events, besides the original creditors, are the credit bureaus; principally Experian, Equifax and TransUnion. Did they maintain verifiable records of people's debts? Mr. McInnis started challenging the credit bureaus to verify the negative credit events in the credit reports of his clients by producing a copy of the Original Creditor's Documentation. He did not challenge the accuracy of these events, just used a legal strategy to challenge the credit bureaus ability to verify their accuracy. In effect, he used Section 609 of the law to demand the credit bureaus justify their reporting. If they couldn't verify the data, they had no right to continue to maintain it on their credit reports. The credit bureaus began to comply. They removed the negative events from the credit records.

The credit reporting agencies don't maintain original document records of credit applications and events. They don't have a signature on a Visa card application. They don't have a signature on a car loan application. They don't have a signature on a bankruptcy filing. All they have are electronic blips in their databases. They simply accept what the creditors have reported to them about debtors. Even though the debtor knows it's accurate, the credit bureaus do not. They can't verify the accuracy of a single piece of data in their database. The credit bureaus are regulated by the government due to the nature of their business, but it's important to understand they are private companies. They are not legally or morally obligated to report anything on anyone. For example, most people know that most negative events remain on a credit report for seven years (ten years for Chapter 7 bankruptcies). This is not a legal requirement. In fact, they could take all bankruptcies off all records tomorrow, if they chose to. They are simply not allowed by law to report these events for more than seven years (or ten). They're not forced to report them at all.

Of course, it's their business. That's why they do it. But they have a choice and when forced to verify the data they report they will choose to take negative events off. Essentially, credit restoration doesn't eliminate negative credit events. It does make them in effect "invisible" to anyone looking at a credit report and this of course is reflected in the credit score.

Chapter Four

Credit Repair After Foreclosure

What a time to talk about foreclosures! It has been the top news at all the leading news agencies for some time and Americans are now experiencing the aftermath of a global crisis. What about the victims of foreclosure? What happens to their credit records? Everyone knows that the recent trend of foreclosures was caused by the economic crisis that affects the entire country, but unfortunately that won't be reflected in your credit report; the credit bureaus never consider 'why' the foreclosure took place.

Repairing credit after a foreclosure is a painful and draining experience. Credit repair needs to be done properly; otherwise, there will be a definite negative impact on all your financial activities in the future. As an example, you might not be eligible for a home mortgage or will have to pay a higher interest even if you do become eligible. Credit repair is a complicated but important process; you need to work on the matter with a lot of determination and consistency. There are three primary things you can do to repair your credit repair after a foreclosure:

- Pay your bills on time.
- Get professional help.
- Establish a budget.

Make sure that you keep track of your payment due dates and that you make your payments before the due date arrives.

Because of the possible complications, you may also want to get professional help for repairing your credit. If you find the right party to help you, this is a guaranteed way to get your credit repaired fast. Without help, you may end up in deeper trouble than what you are already in. Budgeting has also proven its effectiveness in repairing bad credit. You should establish a reasonable budget based on your income and liabilities and stick to it.

You can benefit from credit repair after foreclosure and get the credit rating you want and deserve to secure your financial future.

Fast Credit Repair - How To Raise Your Credit Score In 30 Days

If you are planning to apply for a loan, it would be a good idea to check your credit score and review your credit report. Lenders base their decisions regarding your creditworthiness on your credit score. This being so, you need to ensure that your score is based on accurate information. By taking some simple steps, you stand to raise your credit score in as little as 30 days.

Go over all the negative information on your credit report. The negative items would fall under any of the following categories: Repossession; Foreclosure; Write-off; Charge-off; Settled; Included in bankruptcy; Collection amounts; Court accounts such as liens, judgments, divorce, bankruptcy chapters 11, 7, or 13; Late payments; Inquiries.

Highlight any negative information that you know are inaccurate or misleading. Some common errors include duplicate charges, accounts that belong to another person, or wrong balances.

Write a dispute letter to the credit bureaus concerning the inaccurate information. You have to identify the specific erroneous information, the reason why you believe the information is inaccurate, and what you want the credit bureau to do regarding the error. You may, for instance, ask them to delete or correct the error on your credit report. You need to enclose copies of documentation supporting your dispute, as well as a copy of your credit report with the highlighted inaccurate information.

The credit bureaus are legally obligated to investigate your dispute within 30 days. So, then, you may expect a response from them regarding the matter within that time frame as long as you have clearly communicated the necessary information and provided them with the documentation supporting your dispute.

Aside from taking steps to correct inaccurate information on your credit reports, there are other steps you can take that can improve your credit score within a month's time. One of the things that affect the calculation of your credit score is your debt to credit ratio, that is, the total amount of your debts divided by your total credit limits. If you pay off some of your credit card balances, you would lower your credit utilization ratio. The ideal ratio is just about a third of your total credit limit. Knowing this, avoid using up your entire credit limit. The restraint you demonstrate in your purchases would give a substantial boost to your credit score.

Exactly How to Rebuild Credit After Bankruptcy

When contemplating bankruptcy vs debt settlement it can really seem like a daunting task. But if the decision is made to declare yourself bankrupt then you should be ready to begin putting life back together after this difficult experience. In fact, many people just give up altogether and except a new lower standard of living. This should not be, it is not impossible to rebuild credit after bankruptcy, and much of it can actually be done relatively quickly if a strong plan is put into place.

First one needs to secure shelter after declaring bankruptcy. Renting after bankruptcy can sometimes be a hard task because many land lords require a credit check in order to lease property. One can usually overcome this problem by providing a little extra for a security deposit. By renting this way, one will rebuild credit after bankruptcy as well as secure shelter.

After an individual has a place to live they can then focus on other areas of rebuilding their credit. This can be done by contacting a credit services center. Because of the rising number of bankruptcies that are taking place nowadays professional credit service centers are being made available to help people get on with life and rebuild credit after bankruptcy. These credit centers have can provide useful information to people about how to make the bankruptcy experience less painful as well as how to get personal finances structured in a way that gives them a greater amount of leverage at building their new credit score up.

One technique that can be utilized is to apply for a secured credit card at a local bank. This is a credit card that requires money be put on it first before it can be used. It is similar to a checking account debit card, except that it is tracked by the bank and credit bureaus. Once an individual has established a responsible spending record with this secured card they will be able to have a low balance traditional credit card. This traditional credit card will allow one to rebuild credit after bankruptcy even faster, quickly leaving behind old worries of bankruptcy.

Conclusion

Anyone facing high interest rate loans or increasing rates on their credit cards would benefit from credit repair help. But, knowing where to go and how to employ solid credit repair help can be difficult to track down.

In reality, a lot of people offer credit repair help, but few deliver. The best means for obtaining credit repair help is to make sure you understand your own situation and some good common sense tenants for repairing credit first. If you do understand these things, finding credit repair help will be a snap because you will be able to discern who can help and who can't.

Finding solid credit repair help is a matter of understanding what you need to do to repair your credit. Whether it's paying off high interest rate loans and establishing a better debt to income ratio or erasing errors from your credit reports, knowing these things will guide you in your search for credit repair help. You don't have to be an expert at it, but a basic understanding is important. Leave the expert advice up to the experts if you're looking for credit repair help.

Let's take a look at a few scenarios where credit repair help could come in handy.

Bad credit

Credit repair help in this case might involve the need for a credit counselor to guide you on the path to fixing errors from the past. A person, company or even credit repair help computer program can assist you in targeting reasonable things you can do to improve your scores and pay down debts along the way. It is also possible the best credit repair help you can find in this situation is a consolidation loan to enable the closing of some accounts and the creation of a single, more manageable payment. If you can swing it and your debts are high, this is not a bad route to consider for credit repair help.

Errors

If you need credit repair help to fix falsehoods in your credit report, you will find a lot of assistance out there. There are people, companies and programs that all deal with credit repair help and that can help remove and dispute errors in recording on credit reports. It's also possible the only credit repair help you need is a willingness to dispute the issues yourself. Look into the process and see which route is the best option for you.

While credit repair help will vary in its scope from person to person and case to case, there is good help to be had. Just make sure you have a basic understanding of your own situation and some ideas on how to fix it first. Then turn to the experts for credit repair help if necessary.

Harrison Moore

CREDIT SCORE

SECRETS

How To Raise Your Credit Score And Delete Bad Credit Quickly

Chapter One

What Your Credit Score Really Means

There is a wide range of inquiries encompasses the to some degree strange credit score. That secret is made, to a limited extent, by the very offices who decide the number. Recipes for calculating the scores have stayed quiet, and the numbers are not promptly accessible; at any rate not without accomplishing some work to get them. Individuals frequently need to comprehend what precisely a credit score is, who is behind it, what things sway your rating, and what impact a credit score can have on day by day life. Add to that the intense monetary occasions we're currently in, and your credit rating turns out to be a higher priority than any time in recent memory. We should investigate what a credit score is and how it influences you.

A credit score is simply an endeavour to rank your creditworthiness with a goal number. It used to be that in the event that you needed a credit you would go into the bank, and in the event that you had a decent remaining in the network, or if the advance official had a positive sentiment about you, you could get an advance. Clearly, there is a blemish in that framework; anyone, regardless of how very much regarded, can be an awful credit hazard. Along these lines, by computing the impact of various factors on your capacity to reimburse, the credit offices concocted a way that tries to treat everyone decently.

There are a few distinct things considered by the credit offices when making sense of a score. Fortunately, a large portion of them is good judgment. The one thing that makes up the majority of your score is your instalment history. Along these lines, probably the best thing you can begin doing (or keep doing) is taken care of the entirety of your tabs on schedule. Next, don't owe excessively. Your obligation to-salary proportion ought to be at 25% or less. That implies the sum you owe ought not to surpass 25% of your pay. Try not to open such a large number of records in a brief timeframe, and don't lose an excessive amount of either. Possibly apply for an advance or credit in the event that you genuinely need it. As referenced, a large portion of these things are sound judgment, and they will consistently go far towards improving your general budgetary wellbeing.

Is a credit score actually that significant, all things considered, it's just a number, isn't that so? Right, however, it's an inescapable number at that. The most notable model is the banks. They will utilize your credit score to decide if you get an advance, and assuming this is the case, what terms you will get. Be that as it may, your credit score is utilized by much something other than moneylenders. On the off chance that you go after a position, your potential business may pull your credit report before settling on their employing choice. Proprietors use credit scores to see who they will lease to. Insurance agencies use them as a component of their hazard evaluation before offering you an arrangement.

There is no uncertainty that your credit score is significant. Since you have more data on what it's everything about, you can find a way to maintain or improve your score.

High Credit Score Secrets

There are many advantages to a high credit score that can make life hassle free, but for those who don't have a great credit, fixing is really not a problem. It usually isn't until someone desperately needs a loan or is having trouble finding an apartment that they realize just how important it is to maintain a high credit score. And who would have known that silly late fee at the library had such a affect on your rating?

Good credit will help you quickly secure an auto loan, cash advance or an increased credit limit without hassle. A good score also shows a sense of being able to manage responsibility and make wise decisions in your life. For that reason, your credit score is often used during job interviews, getting car insurance, and even when trying to get new cell phone service.

While a couple relatively small mistakes can drive down you score and prevent you from getting what you need, bouncing back is an easy task. For the do-it-yourself individual, just an hour of cleaning your credit can boost your score as much as a couple hundred points. The results are not only the ability to secure a loan, but to also get an incredible rate that can save your thousands of dollars.

So how do you do it? The secret to having a high credit score is simple. It starts with understanding exactly how this score is calculated. When you know the five things that have the greatest impact on your score, you can manipulate this system in your favor to instantly give yourself a high credit rating.

One example of this is to reduce your debt utilization, which can account for as much as 25 percent of your score. If you are currently using more than half the available credit that has been extended to you, your score will suffer. In other words, if your $5,000 credit card limit currently has a $2,500 balance, the quickest way to boost your score is to reduce that balance.

This can be done be transferring some of that balance to another card in order to distribute your debt more evenly. Another way to accomplish this is to ask for a increase on your spending limit. Both can instantly reduce your debt utilization and raise your credit score.

What Does Credit Score Account For?

Any credit you have will be a piece of your credit report. This incorporates credit cards, vehicle advances, home loans and understudy advances, and so forth. The credit agencies or any planned creditor may utilize this data to produce a credit score. How credit scores are determined is definitely not a mystery by any stretch of the imagination.

Credit Score Explained

A credit score measurably analyzes data about you to the credit execution of a base example of individuals with comparable profiles. The higher your credit score, the more probable you are to be a decent credit prospect. The less insecure you are, the better your odds of getting credit at a lower financing cost.

At the point when a potential creditor takes a gander at your credit report, they are making a gander at a story from in any event one of the significant credit authorities: TransUnion, Equifax and Experian. These organizations gather record and payment data on you from your creditors. Creditors may report data to only one, two or every one of the three credit departments.

It's essential to comprehend what is in your credit report on every one of the three agencies in light of the fact that since certain loan specialists report to specific credit authorities, you may even have different credit scores at every one of the three. In addition, loan specialists don't counsel each of the three agencies either. In this manner, you might be declined for credit by loan specialists that demand data from specific agencies and you may be affirmed by others.

Credit Score Components

Various variables are utilized by potential banks to decide your credit score. A few variables have more impact than others. The most significant factors regarding effects on your credit score result are the individuals who have to do with payment conduct, credit conduct and debt circumstance.

Payment history:

Many of your debt payments are recorded in your credit history, your bill payments, advance payments, credit card payments, store card payments, and so forth, are totally included. Additionally, in the event that you had wrongdoings like late payments or missed payments, the measure of time it took you to address this circumstance will likewise be thought about your credit score.

Extraordinary debt:

This incorporates the sums you owe on your records, the various sorts of files you have and how close your parities are to as far as possible. Overdraft understandings, credit card, adjust, store card charges, credit extensions, and so forth are incorporated inside this classification.

New credit:

This is a significant factor that incorporates what number of uses for the loan you've made and how as of late you've made them.

Credit history: Lender likewise see to what extent you've had credit, to what extent accounts have been open, and to what extent it has been since you've utilized each record.

A brilliant method to improve your credit score is to take care of the entirety of your tabs on schedule, unfailingly! It's the least expensive, quickest and most productive weapon against terrible credit!

Debt to Credit Ratios

When working with people on credit issues and dealing with the complexities of a credit report score, one notices without question that the debt to credit ratio is important. The debt to credit ratio can have a huge effect on that important home or auto loan or that needed business loan. However when balanced correctly, in accordance with the set standards for good credit from the credit reporting agencies, the debt to credit ratio can provide the much needed improvement for your current credit score.

People are constantly commenting on what a good idea it is to make sure and pay off all of your cards every month in full to make sure to establish good credit and show that one can pay their bills. This is such a misconception and only leads to confusion. Having a revolving balance kept at the right percentage compared to your debt and you are on your way to a better credit report.

Learning about your debt to credit ratio can be one of the important steps to putting yourself in the right frame of mind for credit success. For most Americans the debt to credit ratio is to high and it can be hard to obtain any new offers or loans from banks or financial institutions. For example, you have resolving accounts totaling $10,000 but you currently owe $8,000 which gives you an eighty percent ratio, very high for a buyer of a finance deal to even take a second look at you.

Lenders make the bulk of their money through charging interest, not sending out pretty square cards or annual fees. When looking at any model designed for credit scoring, it likes you to maintain your balances and pay over a length of time and it is driven with your ability to do this, amongst other things.

Being a lender in an institution, if I could see that over a long period of time, you had been able to maintain long-term credit worthiness with a company, it would prompt me to want your business and "interest" as well. As a lender, I know the type of customer that I want to solicit my loans to.

Sub-prime Merchandise Cards can be a great way to balance your debt to credit ratio while still warranting that $350 purchase for that lamp you HAD to have at Macy's. Sub-Prime Merchandise Cards are simply cards carrying a line of credit to buy merchandise from a specific merchant which in most cases turns out to be the company who originally sold you the card.

Some marketers, perhaps due to their obvious benefits to the consumer, have started to market these cards while misrepresenting and misunderstanding how they work in their advertising campaigns. Sub Prime Merchandise Cards report to one or more of the three credit reporting agencies and can help to even out your percentages quickly when it comes to debt to credit ratio.

Do It Yourself Credit Score Repair

You can find Ads everywhere for systems, books and secrets to help fix your credit report score in a hurry with virtually no effort. Many of these programs are featured on TV, in magazines and through Pop up ads online. Some of these marketing ads include claims such as the Tabloids use to promote their unbelievable magazines. Claims such as, "Your credit score can jump 200 points in only 3 hours" or "Create a completely new credit file and fix your credit in only a day". The truth is that there is not any credit program that can guarantee results that fast and no quick fix home remedy that will immediately solve all of your problems.

However, with only a little investment of time and effort, you can produce amazing results and raise your own credit score by yourself, without having to pay some credit repair agency tons of money in order to help. Even the Federal Trade Commission has stated right on their website that anything a credit reporting agency can do for you, you can do for yourself. All that is required is making sure to educate yourself properly with the right books and apply some simple techniques to take the time to Do It Right the first time and produce a better credit score.

There are only a few available books that can really help the average consumer to fix their own credit score and these books are well worth the small price. In order to fix your own credit, you need to know not only credit basics, but also the insider tips and techniques that the credit repair agencies use to fix your credit for you. These are easily applied once you are shown how to do it through the right book and using the right letter templates and time-tested methods.

The Credit Secrets Bible is the most highly recognized reading and program in the online search category when I searched for credit help. The publication, first produced in 1994 and with a new edition out by popular demand this year helps people with insider techniques and tips that the credit bureaus don't want you to know.

Credit report can be easy, can save you thousands of dollars and you can do it yourself and make sure to put yourself on a better road to financial freedom. Find out for yourself how simple it can be and read about more of these insider tips to get you started on your credit score education and a better financial future.

Chapter Two

Credit Scoring and Your Financial History

Your credit history affects your ability to borrow and even creeps up to attack how much money it costs you to borrow once you find yourself actually approved for something. Every creditor, lender or individual interested in someone as a prospective customer has a credit scoring system in place to use with the information you provide when submitting your application. An individual's credit report is essential to anyone out there seeking credit and is very important to any loan officer.

Many thinks of credit scoring systems as very vague "Wizard of Oz" type all powerful machines which control your number at a high speed. These credit scores are based on a statistical system however and are as easy to explain as the mystical "wizard". The systems that were created to calculate your credit score use real world data and enable the lender or creditor to view the individual objectively.

Some of these include the number and the different types of bank accounts an individual has, outstanding debts, history of bill paying, debt to credit ratios, any collections accounts that have been brought against the individual, bankruptcies and other factors determined more by the individual and his or her financial portfolio.

By comparing the history and background of one individual against the background of thousands of other consumers with financial situations and payrates that are similar, one can better predict the outcome of a loan offer made to this individual. It is easier to predict future habits based on the person's ability in their past and see whether it is likely that debt will be managed well and repaid in the agreed upon time.

The mathematical system used by credit scoring systems has proven to lenders that it can be a strong predictor of one's future ability to repay their credit or debt to an individual company. The system created was designed to place more emphasis on history and less emphasis on individual statistics, which are variable.

You can request your credit report through a number of ways but it will not help if you do not have the education and knowledge in order to read it and determine what you can do to raise your own credit score. Make sure to arm yourself with the knowledge through the right book, audio tape or program and you can put your credit report to work for you and be on the path to a better credit score.

Credit Reporting and How Your Credit Score is Determined

There are many people out there who are unaware of what their credit score is or how much it already could be affecting their wallet or could in the future if habits are not changed. Lenders have been using your credit report score in determining whether or not to grant you a loan and to calculate your interest rate for some time now. The loan officer knows what a powerful tool for predicting future behavior the credit score can be and has proved over and over again to be.

Credit scores measure risk through mathematical calculations, using statistical research to view each consumer. FICO, which is the most widely used credit-score formula was created by Fair Isaac. FICO scores are now often requested for such simple applications in categories such as cell phone providers, utility companies, landlords and even prospective employers. It seems that your credit score can affect a lot more than just getting that low interest rate on that all important home or auto loan.

Managing your credit score and knowing your score and what is included on the report should be a priority for anyone. First you need to educate yourself on how your credit score is determined and calculated by these reporting companies.

In order to calculate the score of just one individual, FICO credit system uses 22 pieces of data, which they collect from each of the three major credit bureaus and use in their analysis. The system seems to break down into separate categories and then put together a composite of all category scoring into a final outcome. Payment history, types of credit used, current debt, length of your credit history and new credit are the determining factors in credit scoring.

Even though people may think so, income is not a factor in a credit score and does not reflect upon the final score. Individual or variable factors are not taken account in a credit score so that the final outcome is more mathematical and analytical in nature, not using personal feelings or considering circumstance. Credit scores are simply predictors for future behavior based on past experience and behaviors.

The lowest possible credit score to have is 300 with the highest rating an 850. The higher your score is, the lower the possible risk to a creditor, and the better your interest rates are going to be. Having a score that is 800 or above is hard to obtain, with only an average of between 13-18% of the population having an 800 or higher credit rating. The average median credit score is more on average between 700 and 750.

Your FICO score is different from your credit reports. If you want to take a look at your credit reports, this is ALWAYS the place to start when it comes to credit repair. In 2003, The Fair and Accurate Credit Transaction Act entitles you to a free credit report from each of the three major credit bureaus once a year. Make sure to request yours to keep up to date on what is changing on your report.

Staggering when you request the reports also helps you to keep up to date on any changes and staggering the reports will also help you to spot bad information sooner. Many places can help you to obtain your credit report. A comprehensive list is included below to help you to getting your hands on your credit report.

The most detailed information to be found online when it comes to credit scoring seems to be from the creators themselves. You can go to the Credit Education area for the most up to date information regarding your credit report and rights. They offer all three credit bureau's reports, which is highly recommended.

Because credit reporting is based on time and all three agency do not run like clockwork when it comes to which tasks are at hand. When one bureau reports something and when another bureau dates something could vary greatly. It would be impossible for each bureau to keep track of there reports all on the same schedule.

You will find that each bureau has different schedules and ways of reporting which makes it the most advantageous to have all three reports. You want to be able to make sure that all three bureaus show the same things and that one does not report something that the others do not, which is often the case when one bureau receives a collection activity notice and the others don't.

Build Credit History

You can actually build credit history for yourself it is not hard and you can do it quickly and easily. Basically, you have to supply the credit bureaus with what they want. This is an invaluable credit score secret.

It is worth remembering that it isn't only about getting a mortgage when you need to boost your credit, many people from landlords to potential new employees might be interested in your credit history to test if you are a risky investment. As they can't know the real person immediately they will check the report to get an idea of your character.

Make good practices part of your everyday financial dealings and you will build credit history much quicker than you thought. This is how you start credit repair yourself.

1. Obtain a copy of your credit report.

You can get one free copy of your credit report per year and you should do so and then dispute any negative, out-of-date or inaccurate information that is on it. Most people don't even do this first simple step and their credit report gathers all kinds of negative entries over the years. The fact is that you can easily remove items that don't act in your favour if you dispute them. By not disputing them they will always be there acting against you.

2. Add some good accounts.

Some people overlook this easy step. A couple of checking and savings accounts look good on your report. Any potential lender will see this as a sign of stability and they will look more favorably at lending you money. This is feeding them what they want to see.

Use a maximum of 30% of your credit limit. Apply for a credit card if you don't have one. The conditions attached to the card aren't really important you just have to be responsible with it, that is to say use some of the available credit and regularly pay it off. Again you are showing them what they want to see; discipline.

3. Get a loan.

This is a great way to have a variety of credit on your report. You increase your score by demonstrating you can manage different types of credit. Obtain a small loan from a local bank and pay it off.

So, not all credit repair secrets are really "secrets".

Chapter Three

Build Credit Score Secrets

As you enter adulthood, or even if you are rebounding from a string of bad credit blunders, you'll want to build your credit score in order to make your financial life easy. It probably doesn't sound like a fun or necessary thing to do, but it is. Without credit, or with bad credit, you get denied for a job, have a hard time renting an apartment, and getting approved for a car loan can be difficult. It can also be quite costly, as a person without credit is considered at risk to the lender, so they make you pay a hefty premium and interest rates on your loan.

Steps to Build Credit Score

What you want to do is create a credit file. This does by no means hard or time consuming. You just have to do the things you already do in your everyday life a little different.

The first step is to get a credit card. Even though many people will tell you credit cards are evil, they are a necessary evil. Without using credit, you limit yourself from building a positive credit report. All you need to do is get a credit card, use it minimally, and pay it off in full. Lenders like to see that people have extended credit to you and that you know how to use it responsibly.

That means you not only need a credit card, but you need to keep it active. Do not max out your card, just make one minimal purchase enough so there is some activity. Then pay it off. It can literally be a $0.10 purchase if you like. Just keep it active. This will help build your credit score.

If you have bad credit and cannot get approved for a credit card, try a department store or gas card. These are typically much easier to get approved for, but they also generally come with very high interest rates - so be careful with these.

If you cannot get approved for store card, then get a secured credit card. This is a card that is backed by other assets you may have. For example, to get a $500 secured card, you may have to verify that you have $500 cash and set it aside in case you do not pay off the debt. The purpose here is simply to build credit, so again all you want to do is use it minimally. In three to six months the use of your secured card should help you obtain a major credit card without a problem. At that point, you can cancel the secured card.

Secrets to Building a High Credit Score

The advantages of having a high credit score are many; first of all you will have access to cash on demand. You will be able to walk into any lenders office and walk out with as much money as you like for things like cars, credit cards and home loans. In this book, I will go over the secrets to building a high credit score.

The first step to getting a high credit score is taking care of any negative accounts on your report or accounts that may be about to affect your credit report in a negative way. This will involve taking a good look at your credit report and challenging items such as collection accounts, late payments, charge-offs and other derogatory items.

It is important to know that in terms of the credit score formula, a lot of emphasis is put on accounts that are the most recent this is why you want to stop new negatives from appearing on your reports. You might have to settle with collection agencies or get caught up with past due bills to stop the damaging effect they will have on your credit scores.

Once this has been taken care of, the secret to building up your score to a high number would be to create a long history of timely payments on your credit reports. A high credit score means that you were able to take out credit accounts time and time again and pay off the balance without missing payments or defaulting on the loan.

The only way to do this is by keeping accounts in good standing for a period of time. It does require some effort but well worth the effort in the long run.

Easy Steps to a Better Credit Score

Buy a home, drive a nice car, apply for a small business loan -- an impressive credit report bodes well at these turning points in life. The first step to improving your credit is being informed about your financial standing. Once you understand what items are in your credit report you can then work on removing the negative ones. Adding positive items to your credit report is also very important, especially if you have little to no credit history. These few steps should allow you to see an improvement in just 3-6 months. Maintaining good standing in your accounts (both bank and credit cards) will greatly improve your score.

Request Your Report

First things first, where can you go to find out where you stand? There are many sites out there that offer free credit reporting once a year. There are 3 credit reporting agencies that companies use in retrieving your credit report: Experian, Equifax, and TransUnion. Each company's website offers a free trial to show their version of your credit report. Yes, their "version" meaning sometimes one might report something slightly different or not at all. So it is important to check all three versions to ensure accuracy of the information.

It is a common misconception that looking at your own credit report reflects negatively on you and your credit score. This is an absolute fallacy. When you check your own credit report it is known as a "soft credit check" and it is NOT recorded in your credit report nor does it reflect negatively on you in any way. Checking your own credit report is a good thing, and I recommend you do it at least once a year.

Remove Negative Items

There are several factors that could possibly reflect badly on you in your credit report. The most well-known negative element is bankruptcy. Bankruptcy will stay on your credit report for 7-10 years. Avoid filing for bankruptcy at all costs.

The easiest way to do this is to be financially responsible. Don't apply for loans you might not be able to pay back on time and do not charge anything to your credit cards if you don't have the cash on hand to pay more than the minimum monthly payment. Divorce also reflects badly on your credit report.

One of the easier things to remove from your report is a revolving account. Limit yourself to one savings and one checking account each at the same bank. If you have more than 2 or 3 credit cards, then you should strongly consider consolidating your current balances into just a handful of cards. Too many revolving accounts look bad on your credit report, even if they are all in good standing. If you apply for a loan or credit card and you are rejected, do not apply for another one for several months. You are actually less likely to be approved once the rejection appears on your report, and having multiple rejections is very unattractive to others viewing your report. Work on improving your credit and then go back and apply if you still feel the need.

Add More Positive Elements

Now here are some positives that you can add to your credit report. If you currently have little or nothing in your credit history, then I would suggest getting a retail charge card (e.g. an Ox Publishing credit card). One good thing about a retail line of credit is that you cannot use it one a whim. You are only able to use an Ox Publishing charge card to buy books published by them; therefore, you won't use it for an impulse buy, but it is a great way to carefully build your credit. Most popular clothing stores also offer a credit card, but I wouldn't suggest these for most people because clothes are often an impulse buy.

Maintain Good Financial Standing

Monitor your credit report carefully. Each of the aforementioned sites offers constant credit monitoring for a nominal monthly fee. You may also want to check with you banking institution. If your bank offers online banking, they likely also offer credit monitoring.

Top 5 Credit Score Myths

If you've read any number of these articles, you know the high level of importance I place on your credit score and credit score repair. They're like the permanent records your grade school teachers always warned you about come to life. Suddenly, every financial decision you've ever made is under the microscope for lenders and creditors to see should you ever try for a loan.

But there's another side to your credit score - a misunderstood side. Most people don't have the first clue about what exactly goes into their credit score, through no real fault of their own. You can thank the Fair Isaac Corporation for that. They're the company behind the FICO credit scores, the most widely used credit scoring model in the US, and they like to play their cards close to the chest, meaning they don't let consumers or lenders know precisely how they calculate your score.

Since FICO doesn't let anyone in on their secrets, it's up to the lenders and consumers to try and interpret their smoke signals, and that generally leads to confusion. So, in the interest of shining some light on your credit score and clearing up some of the confusion, here are 5 of the top myths about your score:

1. Your credit score is your permanent record. Like I said before, most people equate their credit reports and scores to a report card for adults. And much like a report card and the grades that come with them, a lot of people only think about their scores when they actually see them. If their score is high, all is right with the world. If their score isn't where they thought it would be though, they generally don't feel so hot; some of them even seeing their score as a reflection of themselves.

But here's the thing: just like your grades in school, your credit score can, and usually will change. There isn't really anything permanent about it; it changes every time you look at it. So if you don't like what you see, you can work to change it.

2. Even looking at your score will drive it down. A lot of people who check their credit reports may notice that they have a lot of inquiries on file, especially if they've been shopping for credit in the past few months. While it's true that having too many inquiries on your report can dock you a couple of points per inquiry, those are only the "hard" inquiries - those made by lenders and creditors into your file to determine your financial risk. Anytime you check your credit score yourself, it's labeled as a "soft" inquiry and doesn't ding your credit score.

3. You need a balance to build credit. You gotta spend money to make money. That saying may apply in some cases, but not to credit. You don't need to maintain a balance to build up your credit. According to FICO, only 35% of your credit score is made up of your payment history, and many creditors aren't looking to see whether or not you carry a balance over each month on your credit cards. Worry about keeping current on your bills rather than what kind of balance you should maintain.

4. When you get married, so do your credit scores. While you do promise to stay with your spouse through richer or poorer, your credit score doesn't. Even though your significant other's credit lines may show up on your credit report, and vice versa, after marriage, the individual credit reports remain as just that - individual. Your account may show up on their report, but it remains in your name - only accounts opened jointly affect both parties.

5. Disputing every negative item on your credit report boosts your score. This is certainly a myth I'm familiar with. A lot of credit repair companies tell you that the quickest and best way to dispute all negative items on your credit report. If the credit bureaus don't respond within 30 days, the item will be wiped off your report, and your score will raise.

The problem with that is sometimes (usually) those items come back. Not only that, you could also be taken to court for lying about your accounts, and no one wants that. Rather than fall for empty promises, work on resolving any negative accounts legally, and if you need help, consult a credit repair service that can help you achieve your goals without relying on fast tactics.

Raise Your Credit Score in a Flash

You want to buy the latest iPod. Your kid has been begging for a new PlayStation. Your wife has been hinting about a new set of jewelry. You think it's about time to replace your old film camera with the digital one that everybody's using. Your old cellular phone finally gave up on you. The scene is typical. There are so many things you want to buy, there's just one problem: bad credit score. You can't get a credit card from anywhere. If you only knew how to raise credit score, you'd do it in a jiffy.

If you think there is no one who can help you raise credit score, you're absolutely wrong. Yes, you may be tired of those programs crawling all over the Internet that guarantee to raise your credit score but has no results at all, don't fret. There must be something else you haven't tried yet. Credit Secrets Bible is one of those programs that you see on the Internet that helps you with your bad credit. What makes it different from the rest, though, are the things that it teaches you and the truths about the credit system that you never knew.

How can Credit Secrets Bible help you raise credit score? The credit system is actually full of little secrets, and Credit Secrets Bible exposes you to these secrets. Once you know of these secrets, you will get to see how you can use them to your own advantage. You will get to learn how to repair your own credit yourself, the secrets to start getting pre-approved credit cards in you mail box, learn about scams and what can really help you build your credit. How much you charge and how much you pay each month is also relevant, so you also get to learn about that strategy. You get a copy of a short letter that is guarantees you will never get a call from those collection agencies. You will learn about the "4th largest Credit Bureau" and learn why not minding them may cost you thousands.

You also get to learn the little trick people have been using to double their credit card limits.

With all that and more, not knowing how to raise credit score will be a thing of the past. Raise your credit and get your credit cards approved. Go ahead and start building your credit -- because you deserve the finer things in life.

Chapter Four

Repairing Your Credit Score

You know how important is your credit score for the balance of your financial life. Keeping your credit score high will ensure that the interest rates you pay will remain low. It will also make you eligible for all kinds of loans and credit cards. Everyone pays attention to your credit score, your bank, your employer, your landlord, your cell phone company, everybody. Here are some tips to keep your credit score high and balanced.

Ask for a higher credit card limit

Here's a tip to keep your credit card balance low. The amount of money you owe as a percentage of your total credit limit counts a lot to your credit score. For example if you have a $5000 credit limit and your credit card balance is $2500 you are at the 50% level, which is relatively high. What you can do to reduce your balance-level is to ask for a higher credit limit. For example if you are approved for a $10000 credit limit and you still owe $2500, you will automatically move to a 25% balance-level.

Know your credit score status

Find a way to order your credit reports from the credit bureaus, especially if you are not approved for a loan or for a credit limit raise. It is highly likely that there are errors on these reports. These errors are caused by lack of verification of information the credit bureaus receive from the creditors. Take a good look at the reports and look for these errors. It's up to you to keep your credit report clean so that it will reflect your financial status. You can then write a letter to the credit bureau asking them to correct the errors. Supply any information or documents as proofs.

Build a strong credit history

As time goes by you are building what the experts like to call Credit-History. Your history has a great impact on your credit score. If you have a long history and a positive financial behaviour, then everybody will be more confident and will lend you their money. Therefore it wouldn't be wise to cancel that old credit cards you don't use because you found a better deal somewhere else. The accounts associated with old credit cards remain active and there's a positive credit-history already created for you. Why not use those cards every once in a while to keep the accounts running?

Don't be fooled by credit repair companies

The best way to repair your credit score is to do it yourself. If you don't know what to do and you are ready to trust one of the thousands of credit repair companies out there, then you better think twice. More than half of them are a scam. It seems that everyone and their brother establishes such a company. It's difficult to discover the legitimate ones. Never pay such a company before they provide their services. Always ask information about your legal rights and be aware not to be involved in any illegal activities without even know it.

Make arrangements with the creditors

Sometimes it's a good idea to talk to your lender about that last late payment. Ask them if it's possible to erase it from your credit history. Some goodwill will never hurt you and you'll have the chance to develop a relationship that could be so beneficial for you in the future. If you don't want to talk to the creditor you can write them a letter and express your request in a polite manner. Remember you've got nothing to lose.

How to Improve Your Credit Score Fast With These Secrets!

First of all to understand how to improve your credit score fast or raise your credit score, it's important to know what areas to concentrate on to give you the best results in the shortest possible time.

It's important to have a good credit score for many reasons. Often people don't realize that a score just a few points higher can save hundreds, even thousands of dollars when they apply for and get a home mortgage, for example. If you have a FICO score around 640-660 and you can raise it to a very good score of 760-780, and you take out a 30-year term home mortgage, you would save about $3000 per year. That adds up to $90,000 savings on that same mortgage!

And raising your score may not be that hard for you to do. Going over the following tips and some secrets you may find a few you can apply immediately and see fairly fast results. Even just a few points can make a difference in your borrowing ability and show you how to improve your credit score fast.

1. About 30-35% of your payment history is reflected in your FICO credit score. No matter what happens, make sure to make payments on time. I make mine 4-5 days early online. Making your payment online is important. You know it's not going to get lost in the mail. Also I make the payment early because websites may have technical problems. If you waited to the last minute you may not be able to get into the website. And I think it looks better to the credit card company if you pay a little early.

If you know you'll have enough money in your checking account you can set up automatic payments also. This is good if you foresee any problems with possible emergencies where you might have to go out of town or hospitalizations coming up, etc.

2. About 30% of your credit score is based on how much you owe. If possible try to keep your balances on your credit cards to less than 50% of the limit on each card. The more below 50% the better.

3. Most people don't know that 15% of your FICO score is based on your credit history. So if you have a credit card that is not being used with a zero balance, and have no activity, it can lower your score. So charge something small each month and pay it off so you build up your credit history.

4. New credit. Make sure not to open up any new accounts. 10% of your FICO credit score is based on how many new accounts you open. This also applies to auto or car loan shopping. If you're shopping rates at several companies, do it in a short period of time - within two weeks. Don't drag it out. Making several requests could affect your FICO credit score. It may be better to just get the loan through your credit union rather than have the finance officer at the car dealer shop around. Each inquiry he/she makes is reflected with inquiry marks on your credit report.

5. 10% of your FICO credit score is based on your mix of loans. You probably can't do much to change this except - if you don't have a credit card, get one,

6. Last but not least, if you don't have a credit report, obtain or get a free copy from each of the three major credit-reporting agencies, Equifax, TransUnion and Experian. Go over each carefully and write a letter with documentation if you find any mistakes that are not in your favor.

These are a few of the best ways to show you how to improve your credit score or raise your credit score fast! It really doesn't take that long to raise it a few points and it can make a big difference in your borrowing ability. There are a lot more secrets and trade secrets not included in this short article. With a little more research you can find solutions and repair your credit too.

Surefire Ways to Repair a Bad Credit Score

There are a number of reasons why you may find yourself in a bad credit situation. But whatever the reason for your bad credit, you must find a way to repair a bad credit score. Increasing your credit score and eliminating bad credit records will give you more benefits and freedom.

Here are some tips on how to repair a bad credit score:

Pay on or before due dates. If you want to repair a bad credit score, avoid missed and late payments. A negative record can hurt your credit record and is not a good thing in raising your credit score. Paying on time will add positive records on your credit history and increase your credit score.

Always know your credit limit and your balance. To repair a bad credit score, you should be cautious about your credit limit and balance. Be sure that your credit card company reports this information accurately. Do not go over your credit limit to avoid decrease on your credit score. It is much better if you can afford to pay more than your minimum payment. Keeping your credit balance around 30% of your credit limit will help you raise your credit score.

Always check your credit report for inaccuracies. Detect and dispute any errors as early as possible and contact your creditors to make the necessary correction.

Live within your means. Your goal is to repair a bad credit score, so try to re-structure your spending habits. Live within your means and avoid unnecessary expenses. Make a finance plan around your means and pay your debts on time to build a good credit history.

Read books or seek credit counseling to repair a bad credit score. If you are suffering from a poor credit rating, credit counseling can help you bargain a lower interest rate and improve your credit score.

Credit Score Rating System

Understanding the credit score rating system is of the essence for anyone who uses or wishes to establish or restore credit. And you don't have to know all the intricacies that go into calculating your score; just the basics will do.

The basics of the credit scoring system are not that difficult to understand. This information used to be a closely guarded secret until an act of congress forced Fair Isaac, the creator of the most used credit scoring model, to disclose it. Previously, consumers were forced to fly in the dark, as it were, on something that has such a great impact on their lives.

Defined in simple terms, your credit score is a three digit number that indicates your creditworthiness. Needless to say, a lower score indicates bad risk and a high score indicates good risk.

The patriarch of credit scores is the FICO score as it is the one that most creditors use. And though you typically will get this score when you apply for credit, not all credit bureaus supply it directly to consumers. Only two companies can supply you the real FICO credit score.

The FICO score was created by Fair Isaac Corporation and as you might have guessed, the name FICO is actually an acronym of its creator. It is a number between 300 and 850.

There are pretty few people on either extreme of the score. Most people fall somewhere in between. And it is okay to attempt to attain the perfect score, 850, but it is not all that important and could cause you unnecessary stress. What really matters is the range you are in.

A score of between 720 and the maximum 850 used to be considered prime. But after the mortgage meltdown that started somewhere in 2007 and the ensuing credit crisis the bar was raised. You now need a score of at least 740 to 750 (depending on who's looking) to be considered for the best interest rates in loans, credit cards and other forms of credit.

How is your credit score calculated?

Most of the details of the credit score rating system are still closely guarded secrets. But the basics, which suffice for the average consumer, are as follows:

Your payment history accounts for 35% of your score: A good payment history over a lengthy period of time is what counts here.

You debt to credit ratio accounts for 30%: Maxing out on your revolving credit (such as credit cards) is not a good thing. Fair Isaac considers what you owe on each account as well as in total.

Length of your credit history (15%): The longer your history, the better. This is the reason you should start building credit as early as possible, even after a bankruptcy.

Variety of accounts (10%): A "healthy mix" of types of credit is desired. Also, riskier types of credit such as credit cards often score lower than mortgages, car and school loans.

Number and of accounts (10%): Too few credit accounts can hurt your score as can too many. Applying for new credit frequently can hurt your FICO credit score as it indicates risk (you appear desperate).

You should also be aware that your credit rating will differ with each bureau. This is mainly because different creditors report to different bureaus and therefore each bureau's data can differ from one of or both the twos'.

As if to add more confusion to the whole credit score rating system, each major credit reporting bureau refers its score by a different name. Equifax calls theirs the BEACON score, Transunion calls it the FICO Risk Score and Experian calls it FICO II.

You are not done with the credit score-naming mumbo jumbo just yet. FICO also created what is known as the FICO Expansion Score. This was created for people with scanty history such as recent immigrants. This score considers nontraditional credit data such as utility information and public records.

Think you're done? There is the Vantage score and Next Gen score and more (plus more coming as the credit reporting system continues to evolve).

To avoid the confusion about the credit score ratings system, just go for the score that most creditors use, which is the FICO score. It is worth to repeat that only two entities supply this score directly to the consumers and not all the credit reporting bureaus do. Also, your score does not come free and if it does it is with other strings attached.

Chapter Five

Benefits of Good Credit

Proper credit will allow you to do many things from getting a mortgage or a vehicle, to getting into post-secondary education, getting a great job, or opening your own business. Just as you feel better about lending money to a friend who paid you back quickly the first time, and creditors will be more willing to lend you money when you have a good credit rating. If you are looking to get a loan, having good credit can definitely work in your favor as many lenders will give a better interest rate to people with good credit. With good credit you can also earn rewards points on credit cards that can be redeemed for different things, depending on the card like cash or credit towards a trip. Another benefit to having good credit is credit card companies will offer you higher credit limits. It is not unheard of for some people with good credit to have up wards of $25,000 in available credit on their cards. Of course, you have to be careful with such a high credit limit, you definitely don't want to use the credit if you don't have the funds to cover it or you will be paying hundreds in interest.

If you have already tainted your credit rating, it's still possible to get back to having a great credit rating. It will take time of course, but it's definitely worth doing so you can enjoy all the benefits that having good credit brings. The temptation to borrow money is everywhere, so it takes willpower to say no, but the less credit you have available the less you will use.

If you are in financial trouble and want to get back your good credit rating, there are companies that are ready and willing to help you. Many of these companies are good, sound financial companies, but some are there to take advantage of those seeking help with their debt. It is important to research the company before you sign up for a debt solution company. Go online and check the reviews of the company before you sign up.

Once you find a good, reputable debt settlement company, all you have to do is give them a call and see what they can do for you. They should offer debt settlement, which means that they will work with your creditors to settle your debt; in many cases, for only 40-60 percent of what you owe, because when your creditors know you are in financial trouble they will be more lenient because they don't want you to file bankruptcy. If you do, they will not get paid, so they would rather get some money than none. Find a clear debt solution to help give you an affordable monthly payment that fits your budget, which will get you back on the right track.

Is Good Credit Really Worth the Effort?

Individuals struggle daily to meet their financial obligations, avoiding bad credit by paying their bills on time and working and putting off pleasures to pay interest on excessive debt to achieve good credit. The struggle is truly difficult at times to avoid bankruptcy or home foreclosure, but is good credit really worth the effort? The following article will endeavor to answer this difficult question, and might surprise you.

The real estate bust has left countless households paying off home mortgages that far exceed what they could sell their homes for in the current market, and many others find themselves burdened by high interest credit card debt and are drowning in financing payments with little end in sight. Is good credit really worth it and at what point do the benefits not outweigh the struggles.

Faced with an upside down real estate market many are making the difficult decision to walk away from their homes, downsize and let the banks foreclose.

Bankruptcy, foreclosure, and the resulting bad credit is becoming more enticing than the negatives. Frustrated and upside down, consumers are beginning to ask what were the benefits of their hard earned good credit over the years, as the credit crisis dried up many lending avenues regardless of your credit score.

Your credit amounts to your financial reputation, and there are certainly ethical concerns about walking away from your freely accepted obligations. Loans and credit cards are often accepted willingly, not taking into consideration a possible turn of fortune or unforeseen events. The benefits of good credit include better financing terms, lower rates, easier payoff schedules and approvals for otherwise difficult loans. These benefits can be quite compelling and can make the costs of financing in your life much more manageable.

In current times though, many have found themselves weighing the loss of their good credit benefits with the gains in achieving debt relief from their current herculean debt struggles. If you are overburdened, and your current debt burden seems hopeless, one should not rule out bankruptcy and debt relief solutions that are designed to help. Bad credit and the loss of good credit benefits will result, for a time, but in some circumstances this can still be a sound financial decision.

A struggle to maintain good credit is noble, without doubt, but financial missteps are a part of life. I only recommend you look closely at your situation and do not rule out the possibilities that are available. Bad credit is not the end of the world, and can be improved over time, and everyone deserves a second chance in my opinion. Everyone's financial situation is unique, and cash flow problems can vary, but a sober assessment of your situation is never harmful and sometimes a fresh start is just what is needed.

Maintaining Good Credit After Bankruptcy

How to maintain positive credit can seem like an impossible task to many people plagued by bad credit and debt history. For them the question of whether it is even possible seems tantamount to how to actually do it. Good credit however is nothing difficult, far from being impossible. When understood clearly, credit in itself is no mystery and therefore tackling it is no mystery either. The benefits of good credit are endless and like any self-sustained cycle, having good credit leads to better credit in the future, which is easier to pay off and thereby helps maintain a positive credit.

In order to understand how to maintain positive credit, it helps to know what causes bad credit in the first place. Factors such as tardiness contribute towards giving a poor impression of your finances and will contribute towards a negative credit. When bills are paid late, or not paid at all, it is likely to appear on your financial records. Furthermore, when debts are extended for long periods of time, or accrued to unreasonable extents, they also cause a negative impact. The answer is therefore simple. Paying all your bills on time, well before the due time if possible, and keeping your debt low is the key to maintaining positive credit.

Once you are sure that you are paying all your bills on time, work on paying off any existing debt you may have. It goes without saying that you should limit future debt until all history of debt has been cleared or is well on its way to being cleared. This will help you get better credit, and then any loans or savings you try to get in the future, you will have easier interest rates on them, which will make it more manageable for you. Keeping your debts and bills in check, you should move your focus onto your finance records in general.

Carefully manage and assess all your finances. Even though you cannot see your actual credit score, you can request to see your credit report, which will have a record of all your accounts and finances. Analyze these very carefully for any discrepancies that may exist and be sure to rectify them immediately if you do. If you have many accounts that you do not use, shut them down. There is no need to take on the liability of so many accounts if you are not going to be using them. They only contribute towards a poor credit record.

Finally, make sure you have a well maintained financial and account record. Keep track of all your bills and debt, and work towards paying them off, at a steady and timely rate. Good credit has all the benefits in the world to offer you and bad credit all the harm in the world. Once you know how to maintain positive credit your future finances and decisions should have no reason to suffer, whether you're looking to get a new apartment, a new job, a new home or a new car.

The Advantages of Having a Good Credit Score

There are many advantages and benefits of having and maintaining a good credit score. If you have a credit score of 720, 740, or 760 and up, you have a good score. With high credit scores you will be able to save money each month with lower interest rates on all your financial products.

You will also notice you get a better reception by the car salesmen, home lenders, and even insurance salesmen when you step into their office. They know they have a better chance with closing the sale with you because they can get you approved for a loan at a low rate that you can afford and one that you will be happy with.

A above average credit score will entitle you to demand the best interest rates on home loans, home equity loans, credit cards, car loans, personal loans and more. And in most cases lenders should have no problem accommodating your requests. You've earned your credit now put it to good use.

Another of the advantages of having good credit or good scores to be more precise since you do have to maintain a good score with all 3 of the major credit reporting agencies - Equifax, Experian, and Transunion - is that potential employers will not turn down your application because of your credit history. You stand a better chance of landing a job with a high score as opposed to a low score.

Even if you do not agree with the way most companies use credit scoring information, if you want to get into their game, you have to play by their rules.

And when you do play by their rules, you get to enjoy the benefits of low rate balance transfer offers even when credit is drying up for less than qualified applicants. You still get the perks of being disciplined and not overextending yourself and spending more than you could afford to pay back.

As you can see, there are many benefits and advantages of having a good credit score. To get into the high 700+ credit score range, pay all your bills on time. Stay on top of the due dates like a hawk. Only use a small portion of the balance - less than 25% is ideal. Keep accounts open - 10 to 15 years at a minimum. And don't apply for credit you do not need. Follow these simple steps and you'll be on your way to the best deals on credit anywhere.

Chapter Six

A Good Credit Score Means More Than Just Getting a Loan

When you think of the benefits of having a good credit score, you usually start with how your score affects your ability to get financing. A good score makes it easier to get a loan such as a car loan or mortgage, and it is key in getting a low-interest rate. A bad credit score will make lenders leery of giving you money so even if they are willing to approve your application (something that certainly isn't a sure thing now days), they are going to make you pay more for the loan in the form of higher interest rates to offset the risk that you will default on the loan.

Because of how your credit score gets factored into loans, the simple three digit number that is your score can play a huge role on your overall quality of life. They way it limits or opens up opportunities can determine the size home you are able to purchase, the car you drive, and how much of your earnings go toward assets that increase your overall wealth versus generating profits for the bank (which can affect future big-ticket purchases, your children's education, your retirement, etc.).

But this is not the end of the story. Credit scores which were initially created as a tools lenders could use to quickly determine credit risk, as opposed to digging through each item of your credit reports in an effort to determine your credit worthiness, have been adopted by other industries as well.

Today, not only will your credit score play a role in how your paycheck gets spent, it can affect how much is in your paycheck in the first place. Many employers will use the credit scores of job applicants to aid in the hiring process. Reading through resumes and checking references is a time-consuming process so credit scores are used as a shortcut. Applicants with poor credit scores are viewed as less dependable and trustworthy and will have a harder time even being considered for a position when competing against similarly qualified individuals with good credit. They may not even be given a chance for an interview. Additionally, in certain industries where employees have access to money such as banks, a low credit score automatically disqualifies a person from working there.

Car insurance companies are another group that have adopted the use of credit scores to help determine risk. Studies have shown that drivers with low credit scores are more likely to file insurance claims. And since claims cost the insurance companies money, they want to make sure that the people more apt to file them are charged accordingly. For this reason, the vast majority of auto insurance companies factor in your score when drawing up a policy. The lower your score is, the more you will have to pay in insurance premiums.

Credit card companies also take your credit score into account, which is something most people were aware of, but not everyone realizes the extent of it. Since a credit card is similar to a loan in that you are granted a line of credit that you are required to pay back with interest, it makes sense that credit card companies factor your score into how much credit you can get approved for and at what interest rate. What not everybody realizes is that these figures are not fixed. A credit card companies like to include a "universal default" provision in their contracts in which they reserve the right to monitor your credit reports and increase the credit card interest rate if you have late payments or other negative items added to your credit reports, even if they are completely unrelated to the credit card account. Since credit card debt is unsecured and can be dismissed in a bankruptcy, credit card companies work hard to make sure that if your finances get out of control, they are going to collect as much money from you as possible. Any indication that you might be having trouble making payments and they may start working to offset any future losses.

As you can see, a good credit score opens up a world of opportunities and has benefits many people didn't even realize were there. On the flip side, a bad credit score can be a huge roadblock causing people to have to work much harder in just about every facet of their finances.

Why Bad Credit Lenders Will Need to Adjust What is Considered Good Credit

As a report on your financial reputation your credit score is used by countless bad credit lenders to determine approval for various instruments ranging from loans to credit cards. With the recent credit implosion, economic downturn, and real estate market bust the bad credit lenders will be forced to adjust what is considered a good credit score for approval, helping consumers get approved.

Your consumer credit score is simply an assessment of your reported financial history and your credit is a subjective number used by lenders to determine your credit worthiness. The unintended consequence of the credit and economic implosion is a statistically increasing number of American households with negative marks on their credit reports. Foreclosures, bankruptcies, late payments due to job loss or crushing debt has left many good credit holders suddenly finding themselves with bad credit status.

So how will this affect the market, and what behavior can we expect from lenders in the future? The good news is this ultimately will benefit the consumer. As credit availability increases and the economy turns, lenders will again be in a situation of high competition for potential borrowers. When the tide has turned these lenders will be forced to assess the credit worthiness of their bad credit applicants and will find themselves with a much smaller pool of good credit applicants to lend to. This will force adjustments on the good credit lenders to meet their demands for customers to lend money to as well as the bad credit lenders.

Reversely, credit will become more important than ever. With lower standards because of less availability of good credit borrowers, lenders, as is customary will begin offering more benefits and better terms to the few remaining low risk good credit borrowers. This will lead to lower interest rates, incentive programs, better payoff periods and other perks that can really save you money on your future loans.

So how to best prepare for the direction the loan industry is headed? The wise advice remains the same. Actively work to improve your credit score if you are in a situation to do so, as the benefits make fiscal sense, avoid bad credit decisions if at all possible, and don't beat yourself up if you have had some financial missteps lately, you are not alone. As personal finance times go, this is a time to pick yourself up, dust yourself off, and move forward.

How One Good Credit Consultation Can Save a Life

People are not born with a manual on how to manage credit. As they grew up without good financial education, they often end up in deep credit debt and get scarred for life. A good credit consultation benefits those who want to get out of consumer debt crisis and come up with a rehabilitation plan on how to manage money better.

The proper procedure will not be to jump right away at recommendations for a debt management plan. It is important to trace the milestones that led to the catastrophic personal financial crisis and how the same occurrence can be prevented from happening again in the future. If this is not addressed properly, a vicious cycle of credit crisis might ensue.

A typical output of credit counseling is a sound debt management plan and budget. Both outputs aim to free the individual from credit and get his finances back on track. The immediate debt relief procedure commonly starts with the consolidation of all debts by the individual, negotiation with all creditors for a lower staggered installment payment which the credit counseling agency distributes to a pool of creditors, and a negotiation for a lower interest rate.

Usually banks and other financial lending institutions extend a lower interest rate for those persons who are under a debt management plan. In this case, people who avail of good credit consultation benefit more from the program if they act on their financial crisis before interest and other charges pile up.

There are credit counseling agencies that specialize in this area of personal finance management. In fact, credit counseling has become a separate and distinct industry altogether. There are agencies specially created for profit and there are also non-profit credit counselors that do the job just as effectively. As defaulting debtors steer away from banks during financial crisis, a good credit counseling agency brings the defaulters into a better understanding with the banking and financial concessions without having them get into a direct and heavy negotiation with these banks.

However, according to the statistics of the National Foundation for Credit Counseling, only about a third of those who undergo a debt management plan becomes rehabilitated and is able to stand on his own afterward. The large portion belongs to those who are beyond financial recovery due to a very low income source or simply a lack of financial discipline.

As they say, prevention is better than cure. But if it is inevitable to be under some sort of credit management assistance, make an appointment for a credit consultation with a reputable credit counseling agency. It pays to be an agency one that will save one from drowning instead of plunging deeper into debt. If before, shopping has brought one into a financial crisis, this time shopping for the best credit counselor is highly recommended.

Mistakes To Avoid To Maintain Good Credit Score

Achieving a favorable credit score can take some time for many people, particularly those facing debts. As such, it is wise to maintain it for the long term to enable you to avail of the benefits that go with having a good score.

Being responsible for one's actions is a must especially when it comes to handling your finances. Remember that it's never a pleasant experience to be in debt, to face foreclosure and worse, to go bankrupt. Note that being in these situations can badly impact your life for up to seven years.

So what other mistakes you need to avoid to ensure that you keep your score moving forward. Experts pointed out several small issues that can also affect your score and even lower it into a mediocre number.

Firstly, don't develop the habit of opening too many credit card accounts. The reason is that every application will reflect on your credit report and will elicit a hard inquiry from the agencies. It's true that offers of cash back, rewards points, sign-on bonuses and zero percent interest on new balance transfers can be quite tempting to accept but control yourself and maintain only one or two accounts as much as possible.

Not paying your credit card bill even for just one month is another issue. Did you know that missing a single payment can cause your score to plunge by 100 points? That's right. But then again, you can recover your good standing in about a year's time as long as you pay promptly every month moving forward. This applies for those who have maintained a good credit score. However, those already facing problems before missing out on a payment can expect to recover in more than a year's time.

Closing an account is also not a good idea. Think many times before deciding on closing your old account as this can have an impact on your score.

Some credit card owners are also in the habit of spending up to their limit. But take heed because this is not a good attitude. This will impact your credit utilization ratio and cause it to soar. If ever you do this, though, you have to find a way to pay your balance off so you can still enjoy using the card.

Being in the know about the date your statement closes is also important. But be careful about gaining additional bill before your statement date as this can be reported and affect your score. What you should do then is to try to maintain a low balance before the agency makes a report. If you can, it would be a good idea to pay off your purchases not long after your make them.

You might also want to check your credit report as often as possible. The Fair Credit Reporting Act now makes it possible to get a free yearly credit report. This is essential so you can check for inaccuracies and other errors in your accounts and balances. MainStreet has revealed that 30 to 40 percent of all credit reports have some error with some already hard to correct or remove.

Ways That a Good Credit Repair Service Can Help Your Situation

The fact that you have thought of asking this question before jumping on the bandwagon and trying to get your credit repair is a very good sign. This means you that you have finally started thinking in terms of value for money. There is no fun in spending a lot of money very quickly.

The smart option is to get value worth two dollars for every single dollar you spend. Hence, before you think of employing a good credit repair service provider, just ask yourself - how exactly well I benefit?

From the intangible point of view, the fact that you have a person to whom you can discuss, analyze and reason as far as your credit repair is concerned will be a huge psychological boost. The fact that the person knows more about credit repair and a lot more about financial management than you do will also be an added advantage.

There is a huge difference in discussing these tactics and strategies with your wife and discussing it with a professional who does this on a daily basis for hundreds of customers.

From the tangible and practical point of view, you can get bad credit removed in a jiffy. That is right. There are numerous instances where individuals are suffering from a low score primarily because they have not remove the negative points stated in the credit report.

Once this defect is removed, the credit report automatically witness is arise. Further, a good credit repair service can help you convince the creditor to send this information on to each and every person to whom you have applied for a loan or a job in the past six months.

There are numerous instances where credit bureaus and lenders are try to work together to keep you in the low credit score. The basic idea is to convert you in to sub prime borrower so that high interest can be charged. In such a scenario, good credit repair service can be a huge asset by your side.

You just have to get the bad credit removed by using all the various the strategies and techniques available in the market. Another significant factor is that the credit repair expert will be aware of all the laws and the latest changes that have been made in your favor or against your favor.

All this will help you plan your finances better in the future. If you try to get bad credit removed with the help of an expert, you shall never fail.

Chapter Seven

How to Rebuild a Good Credit History

Having a good credit history is a good thing that everybody will yearn to have, and given the benefits that come with a good history, it is no doubt why many people are rushing to clean up their reports. It is without doubt that one will have easy access to loans and other forms of credit provided the history on one's file shows a good report. But there are some things that are needed to get it right.

First, you need to ensure that you have no negative information on your file. Negative information such as collections, late pays, charge-offs, inquiries, court judgments and other negative entries sends your score down and affects your rating negatively - this is part of what makes up your history. Thus it becomes imperative that you try to get rid of information that will help in boosting your present score and put your history in a good perspective.

But that's not all. You need to take measures to control the everyday active part of your personal finances too. For instance, you may discover that having 4 or 5 credit cards has actually been hurtful to your file rather than beneficial. You might consider cutting some of these cards to improve your rating. But when you're to do this, ensure you keep old credit accounts open and active as the older they are, the better.

Besides this, you should also reduce expenses you make on your credit accounts to between 20 to 40 percent of the total. It is advised you keep your expenses below 20percent for best and rapid results as it will boost your score significantly.

You should also avail yourself of the opportunity to rebuild a good history and rating by signing up with a competent credit repair agency. An alternative method, if you want more control, is to obtain a restoration-kit and do-it-yourself.

Rebuild & Keep Good Credit Ratings by Understanding Your Credit Cards

Secured Credit Card is similar to a prepaid credit card since the funds you are using are actually yours and not the issuer of the credit card. Generally people who apply for secured credit card or prepaid credit card are people with poor credit or unemployed. Prepaid Credit Card spending limit is the amount of money you loaded to the card. There are no interest or finance charges on a prepaid card. With secured credit card, your credit line could be from 50% to 100% of your deposit depending on the institution giving you the secured credit. Therefore the company giving you the secured credit card has zero risk.

Secured credit card can be very beneficial because it gives you an opportunity to rebuild your credit history and you are able to make purchases just as if you had an unsecured credit card. Many companies require that you have a credit card to make purchases, such as car rental, airline tickets, etc. Ensure that the company issuing the secured credit, routinely reports customers' payment history to any of the three main credit bureaus namely Experian, Equifax and Trans Union. This reporting to the credit bureaus will rebuild your credit history over time.

Closing unnecessary accounts and consolidating your bills to make payments more manageable could be an advantage financially. By not applying for too much credit within a short period of time is another factor that will help in rebuilding your credit rating. Additionally, even though secured credit is like prepaid cards, they do have certain fees attached.

Benefits are similar to that of an unsecured credit card, such as usually being paid interest on your balance in the bank, using Automated Teller Machines (ATM) to make deposits, withdrawals, and making purchases at participating merchants. Following the above steps will strengthen your credit rating.

Unsecured Credit Cards are issued to individuals with good to excellent credit rating. Credit ratings depend on certain criteria, such as one's ability to repay loans. These criteria include payment history, employment history, and financial stability. Individuals with excellent credit will most likely receive a lower interest rate. A major factor in maintaining excellent credit is making your loan payments on time thus avoiding late fee penalties.

Customers should read the credit agreement to ensure that they understand their obligation to the creditor. Making payments on time will strengthen your credit rating. Unsecured credit cards has numerous advantages such as low interest rates, high credit limit, business name options, no annual fees, and low APRs on balance transfers up to 12 months. Closing unnecessary accounts and consolidating your bills to make payments more manageable could be an advantage financially. By not applying for too much credit within a short period of time is another factor that will help in maintaining a good credit rating.

Rebuilding your credit takes time, patience, and consistency. If you consistently pay your bills on time, you will see an improvement in your credit ratings over time. There are no quick fixes for improving your credit report except for mistakes or inaccuracies that can be corrected, hopefully in your favor. Your credit information is maintained by the credit bureaus namely Experience, Equifax, and Trans Union for seven years. Therefore poor credit information will remain on your report for seven years. The good thing is that as negative information disappears with positive information, this will definitely rebuild your credit rating.

Applying for secured credit card can be very beneficial because it gives you an opportunity to rebuild your credit history, and you are able to make purchases just as if you had an unsecured credit card. Many companies require that you have a credit card to make purchases, such as car rental, airline tickets, etc. Ensure that the company issuing the secured credit, routinely reports customers' payment history to any of the three main credit bureaus namely Experience, Equifax and Trans Union. This reporting to the credit bureaus will rebuild your credit history over time.

Business Credit Card

Business credit cards are very popular for small business owners because of the many benefits they offer. Benefits includes 0% Intro APR on balance transfers, no annual fees, high credit limit, low interest rates, cash rewards, bonus miles, free online account management to choosing card design etc., At iCreditOnline.com we have some of the best business credit cards from American Express, Advantage, Chase, Bank One, Bank of America, Discover, Citibank, Household Bank and more, with online credit card approval. Why waste time going to a bank when you can get a decision in less than 60 seconds with secure online credit card application. Online Credit Card Approval with Online Credit Card Application is fast and easy!

Student Credit Card

Having a student credit card while still living at home or attending school away from home can be an advantage. It gives the student the opportunity to establish credit at an early age and to start asserting their independence. It comes in handy in case of emergency, it is less trouble and safer to carry a student credit card than to carry cash. Parents find student credit cards to be very convenient. They are able to make deposits to their children's account while they are away from home. Students should be careful with their credit card receipts to avoid identity thief.

If you consistently pay your bills on time, obtaining students credit cards is a good way to established credit rating and start building a good credit history while in school. Establishing and maintaining a good credit rating will make it easy to purchase a car, a home or obtaining a personal loan in the future. For students who are not committed to their financial obligation, getting a student credit card is not a good idea. Running up balances, finding yourself in debt, unable to make monthly payments will destroy your credit rating.

Student's credit cards generally have high interest rates. At iCreditOnline.com we offer some of the best student credit cards from Chase and Discover with 0% APR introductory rate for 6 months, no annual fees and online account access. Online credit card approval with online credit card application is fast and easy!

Explanation of some of the credit cards we offer:

0% Intro APR Credit Card or Balance Transfer Credit Card gives you the benefit of using this credit card without making any interest payment on the principal for a stated period of time. This credit card is marketed to individuals with good credit rating who want to transfer balance from a high interest credit card to a 0% intro APR credit card.

Cash Rewards or Cash Back Credit Card earns a percentage on purchases made. This reward or cash back is credited to your account.

Debit Card takes the place of carrying a checkbook or cash. This card is used like a credit card with certain limitations, such as not being able to rent a car. Purchase transactions are contingent upon having enough funds in your checking or savings account to cover the purchase. Verification of funds requires entering your Personal Identification Number (PIN) at a point-of-sale terminal.

Low interest credit card saves you money. Having a good credit rating qualifies you for some of the best low APR credit card offers.

Prepaid Credit Card spending limit is the amount of money you loaded to the card. There are no interest or finance charges on a prepaid card. Therefore the company giving you the prepaid credit card has zero risk. Generally people who apply for prepaid credit card are people with poor credit or unemployed.

Secured Credit Card is secured by the amount of funds you have in your account. Your credit line could be from 50% to 100% of your deposit depending on the institution giving you the secured credit.

Unsecured Credit Card is issued to individuals with good to excellent credit rating. Credit ratings depend on certain criteria, such as one's ability to repay loans. These criteria include payment history, employment history, and financial stability. Individuals with excellent credit will most likely receive a lower interest rate and can receive instant online credit card approval. A major factor in maintaining excellent credit is making your loan payments on time thus avoiding late fee penalties.

Travel Rewards Credit Card benefits may include travel accident insurance, free rental car collision/loss damage insurance, rebate on gasoline purchases, frequent flyer points or bonus miles towards airline flights, free quarterly and annual account summaries.

How to Qualify For and Establish Good Credit

The credit score shows someone how desirable they are to a lender. When a lender sizes you up to determine how much credit, if any to grant you, it usually looking at your credit report and measures your past credit history performance based on your credit score. Generally, a lender usually looks at these 3 keys areas: character, capacity and capital (sometime known as 3Cs) to project how responsibly you handle your credit obligations. Hence, to qualify for and establish good credit, you need to get good score in these 3 areas. Let discuss it one by one.

Character

When you promptly pay principal and interest on your mortgage, student loans, credit card and other loans, you established a good character. By demonstrating a strong sense of character, you persuade the lender to trust that you will make a good-faith effort to pay your bills even if you run into financial difficulties.

Capacity

Capacity measures your financial ability to assume a certain amount of debt. Whenever you apply for a loan, the lender will ask for your annual income statement and your investment portfolio and he/she also want to get to know your other income sources. Many banks set minimum income requirements that your must meet to qualify for certain dollars of credit. The higher your total earning, the larger your credit capacity will be. Besides considering your sources of income, lender also takes into consideration of your existing debts. They prefer it if no more than a maximum of 36 percent of your income pays your total fixed expenses, and if no more that 28 percent of your income pays for housing, either mortgage or rent. The more debt you incur, the less credit lenders extend.

Capital

Lenders consider stocks, bonds, mutual funds, real estate, collectibles, cars and other asset as your capital that they can disposal to retire your debts if your character and capacity do not prove sufficient. Sometimes, lender may need you to pledge your capital/asset for your loan if your character and capacity are not sufficient to persuade lender to approve your application.

The Benefit of Having Good Credit

Lenders love people with good credit record to borrow money from them. That's why people with good credit get a better offer in applying for credit. Among the benefits of being a good credit are: the lower interest rate, faster application approval, more attractive packages with more choices. It's mean "Save More Money If You Have Good Credit". If you have good credit, you even can negotiate with the lender to lower down the interest else you will turn your head to other lender.

In Summary

Having a good credit score means you have more options available to you. You can get loans with better terms and rates and you have more available to you when it comes to types of loans. The credit record build over time, hence it's never too early to start to establish good credit record for yourself and qualify for better options at the time your need it.

Benefits of Improving Credit Report Scores

If you have ever applied for a loan or opened a new account, you have realized just how important your credit score is. This three digit number is what almost everyone uses to determine whether you are a good risk for lending money to or not. Lenders like to see numbers that are above 700. A credit score of 830+ is considered perfect credit.

However, with so much economic upheaval happening, your credit report may be starting to take a hit. There are many benefits of improving credit report scores. Here's a few things to consider.

Know Your Number

You can't fix something if you don't know that it's broken. In order to start working on improving your credit score, you have to know what is there. While you can get a free credit report, it doesn't show you what that all important number is. In order to find out how companies are rating you, you will need to pay a bit extra to get your credit rating number. However, it is well worth the cost. Also, when you are working to improve your credit score, you need to keep a closer eye on things than a once a year inquiry allows.

It's Not Just About Loans

While it's absolutely true that almost no loan can be cleared without checking your credit report, that's not the only thing that can be affected by bad credit. Any place that requires a background check can pull your credit score. This includes your employer and even your landlord if you are trying to rent an apartment. Poor credit suggests a higher chance of irresponsibility and it can really mess up your life.

Know Your Options

There are several things you can do to improve your credit scores. Refinancing is a commonly used strategy. However, make sure you have a solid financial plan or you'll end up right back where you started. You can also take a settlement or file for bankruptcy. Both of these options will reflect poorly on your credit.

However, if the problem is really bad, it may be worth it. Wiping the slate clean can enable you to start over fresh. Either way, make sure that you keep a close eye on your credit so you can assess the impact of each change you make.

Chapter Eight

Enjoy The Benefits Of A Credit Card!!

Do you need a credit card that has to be applied in your name? If so, how do you go about it?

Are you contemplating on getting a credit card? The answer is very simple. It very obviously is a yes. For most people it is quite necessary to get a credit card as it will help them in quite a few ways. Credit cards have of course transformed our lives to a great extent. Revolution is another pattern it can be seen in. Anywhere & everywhere all you find are ads, in newspapers, TVs, shops, websites and every other place you go to asking you to apply for one. If you take a closer look you will find that most people do own credit cards. Some of them also have many credit cards. Everybody seems to own one. So why can't you?

Although credit cards offer you many benefits, the most important of them all is the convenience which you are given. The sole and the prime reason for getting a credit card will be because of its convenience. A few years back, when not many accepted credit cards this was not a good choice. But in today's world it is quite convenient to own one. Carrying lots of money on you might be unsafe as well as inconvenient. This is when a credit card which is a small piecemade of plastic can be very attractive. You will not need to keep paying the bills till the next months billing cycle. So buying when you want is possible even if you don't have ready cash on you. A great reason to apply for a credit card is that you can buy now and then pay them later. Merchants also offer you an installment payment plan which is interest free that is when you can make a very big purchase and keep paying it off in regular installments. Hence credit cards work as long term loans. You will be also entitled to discounts on your shopping with credit cards. Tie ups are made between the merchants and the credit card companies. These are indeed quite a lot of benefits that a credit card can offer.

There are many methods in applying for a credit card. You can either do it over the phone (by getting the representative to make an appointment with you), the net or applying it in person. A lot of representatives will be asking you to apply with their company. To get a credit card you will need to fill an application form which will be quite easy as you will have an assistant in guiding you. By filling this form you will be agreeing on all their conditions as this form is actually an agreement form. You will receive your credit card as soon as this is done and your credits are checked by the company you signed with.

It is not a compulsion for you to apply for one. But for most people who do not have a credit card, it is highly recommended you apply for one as soon as possible.

Making a Good Credit Card Comparison

Many people are into the fray for the need for a credit card for some reason or the other. It is also a well known fact that before choosing a particular card you need to do enough research and make enough enquiries. But what many are not aware of is how to make a credit card comparison which is very important in deciding on the best card.

How To Find The Best Credit Card?

Today the market is filled with companies that are ready to offer cards to people and in order to attract customers they make many attractive offers. As a customer it is your duty to conduct complete research and find out how authentic and useful these offers are. In order to compare cards you can check online ratings given to card companies. These ratings are based on many findings and therefore you can trust them to make decisions.

On the net you can also find sites that are put up by other banks and financial institutions in order to help customers to get necessary information on companies offering credit cards. These sites also provide the facility of getting rates from other companies which facilitates comparison. They also give details of card deals that are offered by the companies and the most popular one being the 0 interest cards that are very helpful to customers.

What You Need To Be Careful About?

Making a choice of the credit card is very difficult due the presence of numerous credit card companies. Your choice should also depend on the use of the card in your special fiscal situation because there are many cards that serve different purposes. If you are aware of that then you can choose the right one easily. One type of card that is very popular these days is the card that allows transfer of balance from one card to the other. This card is very popular because of the amount of money that can be saved by the user. The facility is also offered by the low interest credit cards. These cards facilitate savings and therefore people prefer to subscribe to such cards.

With the fierce competition that exists among the many companies, it is interesting to view the offers and then make a choice as most of them are at par when it comes to the facilities offered. All you need to do is to keep your eyes open to all the available information regarding the benefits and offers offered by the companies and you are bound to get a card that suits you best.

This form of awareness and caution is necessary, failing which you could get a card with minimum offer and maximum charge and you could be stuck with it for life. Making good credit card comparison helps a lot in benefiting from a card that is more of an asset. After all it is your savings that are going to be affected by the purchase.

The Benefits Of Accessing Credit Reports On A Regular Basis

Credit and debt have become the norm. If you were to look around your neighborhood and take stock of the homes and cars people have you may think that you are living in a prosperous age. In actuality, most properties and vehicles today are not bought outright, they are obtained through loans and lines of credit.

Every individual has a credit rating and report. Though this information is not usually seen by consumers, it is always analyzed by lenders prior to the granting of a financial service. If your report was to contain information of a somewhat negative nature, this will have a serious impact on your ability to acquire loans and related services.

By accessing your personal credit report, you can take stock of your current standing. Not only would this allow you to understand how easy it will be to be granted a new loan, you can also ensure that your identity is not being used for fraud. Unfortunately, many people fall victim of ID fraud and are unaware of the problem until they apply for a loan or similar service and are refused due to unexpected bad credit.

By regularly monitoring the information kept on file in relation to your financial standing and monetary obligations, you can help reduce the risk of falling victim to ID theft. What's more, there is always the possibility of creditors and lenders making mistakes. By going to the effort to read all the entries in your report you can ensure that you are not going to be viewed unfavorably unnecessarily.

If you are to request a report to be sent to you, you will need to know how to properly analyze the data that it contains. Most feature four sections: personal information, score, account history, and inquiry information. Each section contains valuable entries and should be checked carefully. If you are concerned about fraud, the account history gives an indication of the different loans and agreements that have been taken out in your name.

A personal credit report is a document that everyone should access at least once a year. No matter what your current financial situation is, regularly checking the financial account information that is held on you can help combat identify theft and also allow you to make informed decisions in relation to applying for loans and similar services. Though there is usually a small fee involved with accessing a report, it is money well spent.

Rebuild Your Credit With A Prepaid Credit Card

It can be pretty tough when your credit is bad and it is next to impossible to get credit when you need it. Most major credit card companies will not talk to you, and a lender - well, forget about it. There is a way, though, out of the tough situation with a prepaid credit card. Here is what you can do with a prepaid credit card to help rebuild your credit score.

Need A Bad Credit Rating

One of the best things about a prepaid credit card is that it was designed for people with bad credit. In fact, that is one of the qualifications. There will not be any check on your credit rating, or your employment. Anyone can get one of these credit cards, but you will need to deposit a cash amount equal to the credit limit you want. This lets you know that it operates on a debit basis - no actual credit is given.

Get A Card That Reports To A Credit Bureau

Not many prepaid credit cards actually report to a credit bureau. That is, however, the kind of card that you want to get. While others make having cash handy, it really will not help you (or anyone with bad credit) in the long run.

Watch The Fees

Prepaid credit cards often come with a number of fees. You should compare one card with another in order to get the fewest fees. In order to get a prepaid credit card that reports to a credit bureau, you will probably have to pay an annual fee - could be as high as $100.

Look For Benefits

Most prepaid cards do not come with any benefits, but some do. You can get points, like on a regular credit card, that are useable for a few benefits - like free phone time, and more.

No Credit Card Abuse

Another good thing about these credit cards is that you can never go over your limit, or have to pay any late fees or interest. (Hey, this is sounding better all the time). This means that if it reports to a credit bureau, that it would be impossible to get a lower score than what you may already have with this kind of card.

Easily Put Cash On Your Card

Most prepaid cards will allow you to easily put credit on it from just about anywhere. You can even put your paycheck onto it by Direct Deposit.

Use It Like A Credit Card

A number of these prepaid credit cards can be used in the same way as a credit card. You can set up automatic bill payments, purchase things online, or over the phone. If you want this feature, however, be sure that the ad says that you can do this.

Like any other credit card, you will want to compare features and fees in order to find the best prepaid credit card for your needs. While most of them are similar, the fees vary widely. Since no qualifications are needed, why not get the best?

Help Find The Best Credit Cards Rates By Researching Credit Cards Comparison

If you have been turned down for credit in the past and you want to be able to get financing to buy something. We help show people how to compare different offers to find the best credit card to fit their needs. Depending on why you are looking for a credit card. You need to first learn about the benefits that you can pick from based on what is important to you.

Your credit score is the primary factor that determines what kind of credit card deal you can get approved for. There is a way to repair your credit just by disputing all the negative things that are on your credit report. You would be surprised at how easy credit repair is. All you have to do a lot of times is just initiate a dispute about any bad item on your credit report. If they don't address your request within 30 days then it has to be removed from your credit report legally. This doesn't matter if the information is true or not. Most of the time that is all it takes to get bad items removed from your credit report.

Your personal credit report is your property you have the right to dispute information on that report that can be used against you. This helps you get a better deal when doing credit cards comparison. The credit bureaus want you to have bad credit. The lower your credit score is the more money the banks make when they lend money to you. All these institutions work together. So this means you are guilty of any and all information that is reported about you to them until you prove your innocence. The problem is no one tells you that you even have this right to repair your credit. It is not to the best interest of the credit bureaus or the banks that lend money to hand out this information.

If you want a new credit card then you will want to look at the benefits of the card that you want. You can choose from things like low interest credit cards, balance transfer credit cards, cash back credit cards, bad credit credit cards, and much more. Look through our guide for credit cards comparison to find out what kind of credit card you would like to have.

Credit cards are a great tool when financing things that you need. They are no good to you if all you plan on doing is shopping for things that you can't afford. This is what gets people in trouble as most of us know all to well. Now if you are financing just 1 large purchase that you want to make payments on. Using a credit card for that would be a smart thing to do. Or if you just want to earn rewards on things that you need to buy regularly like buying gas. You need good credit to get approved for these kinds of credit card offers. So if your credit isn't that great and you want to repair it. Check out our guide for easy credit repair. This will give you more information on how you can raise your credit score so you can get approved for these kinds of credit card offers.

Is it Possible to Improve Your Credit Scores and Live a Normal Life?

A low credit score can really be bothersome when you need to rent a home, get an installment loan, or just about any type of loan. Creditors usually look at your credit report and if your it is below the ideal 660, they will tend to reject your application. The worse news is that this rejection is still another reason for your score to sink further.

If your whole financial world revolves around credit cards and loans, you have to realize that your credit score is the bottom line of all your financial transactions. It affects how much interests you pay on your cards. It also determines the amount of money you have to pay on your other bills wherever you may work or live in this country. It makes sense these days to improve your financial standing Failing to do so will greatly reduce your chances of getting advantageous interest rates. Your score is reviewed by loan companies and banks before they allow you to get hold of their money. A low score means higher interests. If you need to get a loan for a car or have to get home insurance, or even a cell phone service, a high credit score will get you lower premium payments and a better package for services you require. Even landlords can check your finances, as well as employers before accepting a prospective employee.

So how do you improve your credit standing and still live a normal life? It would seem that you will always be under scrutiny every time you transact where credit or loans are involved. Borrowing and loans are a privilege but you need to use them properly to benefit from it. By setting your mind firmly on this belief, you can begin to improve your credit rating slowly but surely.

For most people, their first credit card is the genesis of their credit history. This is good because a longer credit history is a plus when calculating your scores. However, applying for many credit cards can actually lower your score since each credit inquiry will cost you up to five points. It may seem like a good idea to get a card from a company that will not report your credit limit to the established credit bureaus or doesn't give you a spending limit but this is actually a sure way to hurt your credit score. If you already have several cards, don't cancel them all at one time. Doing so can lower the credit available to you and deduct points from your credit score. Try to keep old credit cards and use them from time to time in order to maintain a long credit history which can help a lot to improve your credit scores. And keeping your credit card balance lower than 30% of your credit limit will also be a great help.

All credit gurus are unanimous in saying that paying your debt always on time is the best way to improve your credit scores. One late payment is all it takes to ruin your credit score - a deduction of as much as 100 points and it stays on your credit report for seven long years.

Books by the same Author:

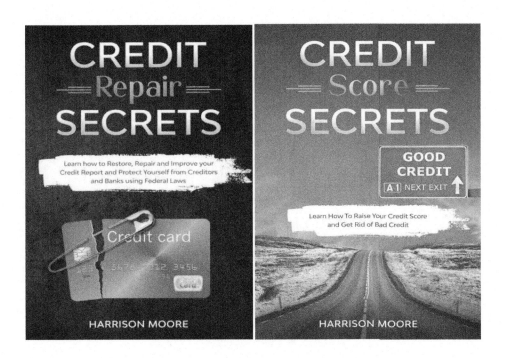

Search: "Harrison Moore"

at Amazon

Kind reader,

Thank you very much, I hope you enjoyed the book.

Can I ask you a big favor?

I would be grateful if you would please take a few minutes to leave me a gold star on Amazon.

Thank you again for your support.

Harrison Moore

Printed in Great Britain
by Amazon

26773577R00090